TALKS MY FATHER NEVER HAD WITH ME

(Helping The Young Black Male Make It To Adulthood)

By Rev. Harold Davis

©1995 by
Rev. Harold Davis
KJAC Publishing
P.O. Box 111
Champaign, Il. 61824

Additional books may be ordered by writing the above address or calling **1-800-268-5861.** Rev. Davis can be reached at Canaan Baptist Church 402 W. Main St., Urbana, Ill. 61801, 217-367-2158.

All Scripture quotations are taken from the 1611 Authorized King James Version of the Bible.

ISBN0-9638553-1-X

Graphic Design by Carlton Bruett
Photo by Chris Brown

Printed in the United States of America

Dedication

This book is dedicated to John Thomas Davis (1904-1993) who taught me by precept (teaching and rules) and by practice (example). It is his consistent, continuing influence in my life that has made me the man that I am today. Although his head is cold in the grave, his voice still resounds loud and clear with counsel, correction, rebuke, and encouragement that helps me on a daily basis. Thanks Pops.

Special Thanks to:

- Dr. Ollie Watts Davis, my wife, counsellor, friend, lover and the mother of my children;
  Whoso findeth a wife findeth a good thing, and obtaineth favor of the LORD. Proverbs 18:22

- Rev. B.J. Tatum, my pastor with strong shoulders;
  Let the elders that rule well be counted worthy of double honor, especially they who labor in the word and doctrine. I Timothy 5:17

- Rev. Dr. Edward Copeland, my brother in the ministry;
  Iron sharpenteh iron; so a man sharpeneth the countenance of his friend. Proverbs 27:17

- Rev. Matthew Julius Watts, my brother in the ministry;
  Iron sharpeneth iron, so a man sharpeneth the countenance of his friend. Proverbs 27:17

- Kirstie, Jonathan, Ashley and Charity, my wonderful children whom I love and squeeze daily.
  Lo, children are an heritage of the LORD: and the fruit of the womb is his reward. As arrows are in the hand of a mighty man; so are children of the youth. Happy is the man that hath his quiver full of them: they shall not be ashamed, but they shall speak with the enemies in the gate.
  Psalm 127:3-5

Note To The Young Black Male

This book is designed to make you think and consider many things. Young men throughout the ages have had a tendency to make many of the same mistakes. If you can avoid these mistakes you will have a better chance at being successful in life. As you read these pages consider your life and how you can apply what you read to your life. If you disagree with a point made in the book, find an older wiser man to discuss it with. Lastly, I challenge you to read the Scriptures included in each chapter because they will have a supernatural effect on your life. (I know I'm right about it)

A Note To The Older Black Male

This book is designed to be a tool that will enable you to interact with a younger man and instill in him solid proven principles for success. I challenge you to schedule a time once a week to spend with one to three young men to read and discuss the book together. The young Black male of today is gifted with many talents and in most cases possesses an untapped potential lying dormant in his soul. The topics in this book are designed to stimulate conversation and open the door to more topics of discussion which will surface as young men open up and share their concerns. When the young men open up, you can share from your rich experience, which will impact the young men greatly. Let me make some suggestions:

1. Pray and ask God for guidance.

2. Select up to three young men, maybe total strangers who are in need of guidance. Please note: in most cases the young men are not aware that they need guidance. If there is no father in the home or any form of dysfunction, the young man is a good candidate for your attention.

3. Explain to the young men that you are conducting a series of Black male enrichment sessions and as an older Black male, you would like to spend some time with him.

4. Secure a meeting place (home, Church, community center, or a park).

5. Plan to read and discuss 1 or 2 chapters a week, incorporating a social activity or two along the way such as a ball game, amusement park, McDonalds or visit them at school. Be creative!

6. Ask the Holy Spirit to give you wisdom as HE ministers to the young men through you.

7. Don't gloss over the Scriptures because they will work supernaturally in the lives of the young men.

8. At the end of the sessions, seek to involve the young men in a local Church's young men's fellowship. If the church doesn't have one, **START ONE!**

9. To God be the glory. Give Him the credit. Amen.

Contents

Preface

IF YOU ARE A YOUNG BLACK MAN FROM age of 9 to 19, the odds are against you surviving reaching age 40. There are many reasons why this has to pass. I sincerely believe that if a young man will att to understand the bigger picture and the destructive forces come against him from many directions, a strategy ca developed to help overcome the hurdles.

This book seeks to provide young men with perspective that helped earlier generations survive aga tremendous odds such as illiteracy, slavery, prejudice a poverty. There is a source of tried and true wisdom availal that can help today's generation of young Black men not on survive, but excel in our contemporary society.

A recent study has shown that of the Black males aliv today, 70% will not be around in twenty years. This statisti points out the destructive lifestyle that has been adopted by large number of our young Black men. Each young man that dies or is put in jail is someone's son, brother or father. For families, statistics are irrelevant but the loss of a relative is very significant.

This book attempts to address areas that the author feels we should strengthen in our young men in order to prepare them to live a successful and productive life. The questions at the end of each chapter are designed to provide a tool for discussion between older men and younger men.

Introduction

THERE WAS A TIME WHEN FAMILIES LIVED together in what was called an extended family. Parents and grandparents were close at hand until they passed away. I remember my grandmother being around to give me advice and correct me when I was young. We all need wisdom to live above our circumstances and the best wisdom comes from God. The next best wisdom is wisdom that comes from older people who have been talking to God. This is what we are losing in our contemporary culture.

This book attempts to provide some Godly advice on contemporary issues that may not be available to many young men today. This type of wisdom and common sense advice is of the father-to-son type. It would be received while riding in a car, walking in the park, fishing, or hoopin'.

So, let us begin our time together, in the park, discussing some pearls and principles for living.

PART ONE

I AM WHO I AM

CHAPTER ONE

The Importance Of
Understanding Your Orientation

THERE ARE SOME FUNDAMENTALS THAT A person needs to understand in order to be successful and stay successful. Fundamental number one is an understanding of how you were raised, and what those who raised you did right and what they did wrong. This is called YOUR ORIENTATION. **Gaining an understanding of your orientation is important because it will provide you with objectivity (fairness) when dealing with yourself and others.**

A few years ago I purchased a run-down house that I intended to remodel and rent out. There was a lot of damage to the house, much of which was visible to the naked eye. What I did not know was that there was additional damage that I could not see. Not long after buying the house, I found out that the foundation under the middle wall of the house was cracked and sinking. It required going under the house, digging around the foundation and reinforcing it. It was very hard work, but necessary to make the house safe and liveable.

Your orientation is your foundation (how you were raised.) It is what your life today and tomorrow is built upon. In most cases, foundations are covered up and not seen once a house is built. This can be tragic because some of our foundations (orientations) are faulty and need to be re-examined. As you read the next few pages take a shovel and remove the hard soil from around your foundation and take a close look for cracks and defects.

My earliest memories are pleasant memories of spending time with my dad. My dad was and is a source of and wisdom that has been with me through the years. He always had time for me and though he was not extensively verbal, (he did not talk a lot) he did give me many insights into human nature.

On one occasion when I had a business deal go sour, he heard me angrily tell the person over the phone that I was on my way to see him and that I would discuss the matter with him when I got there. My dad informed me that you don't tell people that you are coming over to discuss an issue with them, for if you do that, they will have time to prepare a defense. The way to do it is, to just show up and discuss it with them. Then, you have a better chance at success. I appreciated my dad's advice. Because of my relationship with my dad and watching him for years and years, there are some benefits that I picked up from being around a wise older man who loved me.

It was not until I was grown that I began to understand the impact of my relationship with my dad. I contribute my desire to work to my dad. He modeled a strong work ethic for me. I learned at an early age to hustle because I saw my dad hustling. I thought that all men hustled. My dad never argued with my mother even though he did get frustrated with her. As a result of living in that environment, I don't fuss and cuss with my wife and to my knowledge, none of my brothers fuss and cuss with their wives.

I don't know what your orientation has been, but one thing is for sure, I do know that it has affected you greatly. You are what you are largely because of your orientation or upbringing. There is a saying that if a child is raised with criticism he learns to criticize, if he lives with hostility he learns how to be hostile. As a parent of four children, I am amazed at how my children have picked up the characteristics of their parents. My children are all musical, so are their parents, my children are all spiritual, so are their parents.

There are many other characteristics that they have acquired as a byproduct of growing up in our house. I know of unfortunate cases where the parents are doing all of the wrong things and their children are acquiring these traits as well.

Many males wait until they are 40 years old before they start to examine and correct the mistakes their parents made in raising them. Please note that there is a proper way to raise children. If the children are not raised properly, there will be forms of dysfunction that follow. What I mean by dysfunction is that something in your family is not working right, such as divorce, abuse, violence, extreme poverty, drugs, crime, hate, shame, guilt, and the list is endless. If you want to get ahead in life, you need to start studying yourself (your orientation) now.

Only <u>YOU</u> can figure out why you act the way you act and do the things you do. Only <u>YOU</u> can change you.

Here are some things to consider and think about:

1. WHAT MAN HAS SERVED AS YOUR ROLE MODEL WHILE YOU WERE GROWING UP?

Every male is exposed to older men as he grows up. These men may be family members, neighbors or friends, but we all have had men in our lives that we learned from. Now that you are getting older, do you recognize the bad habits that you observed these men display that you should not copy? Have you noted how an older man's mistakes and bad choices have hurt him? Have you determined to avoid at all costs the traps that scarred his life?

My main role model was my father who was a wonderful man and wonderful father but he still was not perfect. There are habits that my father had that I fight whenever I see them developing in me. Are you fighting all known negative influences?

2. WHAT WERE YOUR ROLE MODELS' COPING MECHANISMS?

What did your role model do or turn to when he felt like he couldn't make it? Did he turn to alcohol, cocaine, marijuana, cussin', hittin' somebody, fussin', staying out late, prayer, or driving the car fast? There is an old saying: "Like father, like son" which has proven to be true in many instances. Older men make grooves, ruts, and paths in which young men follow. Sometimes it is very difficult to avoid these paths made by the men who went before us. **Coping mechanisms** is an area of need in the Black community. Men need to learn to find strength in the hard times without turning to drugs, abuse, sex, or running away. In the past, men coped by doing positive things, such as working hard, basketball, prayer, talkin' it out, or dancing. Recreation served as an outlet to relieve tensions.

Today many of these coping skills have been pushed aside for coping mechanisms that are destructive to the man, his family and the community. All young men should learn to develop a variety of coping mechanisms that will provide strength when times get hard. I would like to suggest that all young men do these things:

A. PRAY FOR AND SEEK TO DEVELOP WISE CLOSE FRIENDS WHO CAN HELP YOU KEEP PERSPECTIVE WHEN YOU ARE HAVING HARD TIMES.

I have wise men that I can call day or night if I am having a problem and they will give me a word of wisdom when I can't seem to think. Did you know that when you get mad that your thoughts are not always in your own best interest? So, it is wise to have other men to help you think when you get mad. Have you ever noticed that on the basketball court when the defense gets a player surrounded and he is clutching the ball, trying to get free, the other team mates will yell: "Throw me the ball!" As simple as that sounds, we often forget to throw the ball and we also forget that we have someone to throw the ball to.

> *Faithful are the wounds of a friend; but the kisses of an enemy are deceitful.*
> *Proverbs 27:6*

> *Where no counsel is, the people fall: but in the multitude of counselors there is safety.*
> *Proverbs 11:14*

B. AVOID ALL INEBRIENTS (drugs).

Avoid the gateway drugs such as cigarettes, marijuana, beer and wine. These drugs only lead you to harder drugs. That is why they are called gateway drugs. Get wise to the TV commercials that show young, athletic people drinking and go look in the alley at the drunk and see reality. One drink is too many and one thousand is never enough.

> *Who hath woe? who hath sorrow? who hath contentions? who hath babbling? who hath wounds without cause? who hath redness of eyes? They that tarry long at the wine; they that go to seek mixed wine.*
> *Proverbs 23:29-30*

C. SEEK THE WISDOM THAT GOD OFFERS.

God says that if you ask for wisdom He will give it to you.

> *If any of you lack wisdom, let him ask of God, that giveth to all men liberally, and upbraideth not; and it shall be given him.*
>
> > *James 1:5*

There is a difference between man's wisdom and God's wisdom. It is most beneficial to seek God's wisdom. I have met young men in their late teens who have done this. They have displayed the wisdom of forty year old men.

> *Happy is the man that findeth wisdom, and the man that getteth understanding. For the merchandise of it is better than the merchandise of silver, and the gain thereof than fine gold. She is more precious than rubies: and all the things thou canst desire are not to be compared unto her. Length of days is in her right hand and in her left hand riches and honor.*
>
> > *Proverbs 3:13-16*

D. LEARN HOW TO HANDLE YOUR ANGER.

Anger is a God-given emotion that is designed to protect us, by keeping us and our world pure. Appropriate anger results when helpless people are abused or righteous standards are violated. Anger was never designed to destroy us but that is what it will do if we do not learn how to handle it. Always seek to think before you talk when angry. Avoid getting physical when angry because angry people are out of control and hurt others while angry. Walk away from a situation that has made you angry. Realize that you don't have to fix the situation right now. Take time to analyze yourself to see what role you played in causing your anger.

A wrathful man stirreth up strife: but he that is slow to anger appeaseth strife.

Proverbs 15:18

E. WORK ON FEELING GOOD ABOUT YOURSELF SO THAT YOU ARE NOT CRUSHED WHEN YOU FAIL.

The ability to keep standing when everything around you has fallen is the key to success. How you feel about yourself will greatly determine if you keep going after failure. Your orientation and how you deal with it holds the key to your future. (The question on the floor is:) "Are you man enough to look at your past, embrace the good and eliminate the bad?" We really don't have a choice. I challenge you to use wisdom and deal with your orientation because when you do, the sky is the limit when it comes to your future. For the following questions, you may choose to use a private sheet of paper or you may choose to discuss this section with an older man or a group.

QUESTIONS
FOR INTROSPECTION AND DISCUSSION
(to make you think)

1. List five men who have contributed or are contributing to your orientation, personality, morals, habits and future success.

   A._____

   B._____

   C._____

D._____

E._____

2. List five negative events from your orientation that have damaged you and need to be dealt with in order for you to function properly.

A._____

B._____

C._____

D._____

E._____

3. Give yourself credit and name some negative things from your orientation that you have faced and conquered.

A._____

B._____

C._____

D._____

4. List five qualities that you would like to eliminate from your personality, or habits that you would like to drop.

A._____

B._____

C._____

D._____

E._____

5. State to yourself and another person when you plan to start eliminating these negative qualities and the practical steps you plan to take to accomplish your goal.

_____

_____

_____

_____

_____

APPLICABLE SCRIPTURES

Train up a child in the way he should go: and when he is old, he will not depart from it."
                                            Proverbs 22:6

I can do all things through Christ which strengtheneth me."
                                            Philippians 4:13

Examine yourselves, whether ye be in the faith; prove your own selves.
                                            II Corinthians 13:5a

The heart is deceitful above all things, and desperately wicked: who can know it?
                                            Jeremiah 17:9

And I will restore to you the years that the locust hath eaten, the cankerworm, and the caterpillar, and the palmerworm, my great army which I sent among you.
                                            Joel 2:25

CHAPTER TWO

Ask Yourself The Question: "Have I Been Properly Nurtured?"

Y OUNG MEN NEED TO COME TO GRIPS WITH the fact that there may have been something missing in their upbringing. If you are the type of person who needs attention, feels unloved, and maybe suffers from low self-esteem, it is possible that you were not given enough attention as a child.

I was at a friend's house one day visiting with him and his wife. We were involved in an adult conversation that we were enjoying very much. Our conversation was interrupted when his six year old daughter walked into the middle of the adults who were sitting around and spoke her mind. The child said: "I'm not getting enough attention." She was displeased with her parents' temporary abandonment of her needs to meet the needs of their guests. What I found most interesting was that she verbalized her concern. She didn't trip or act out her frustrations like many children and adults do, she very calmly said: "I'm not getting enough attention."

I like her approach. Some of us need to admit that we are not getting enough attention or we did not get enough attention when we were younger. Have you experienced what it feels like to be loved by a father or a father-like person? Have you experienced the comfort of knowing that your dad would protect you from danger? Have you experienced the assurance of knowing that dad would be there no matter what happened? Did you receive objective, (fair) well-balanced discipline? Was there a grandmother or auntie in your life who offered you unconditional love and discipline? What amount of nurturing did you receive as a child?

As a child, my best friend was my white, female collie named "Bootsie". I loved Bootsie with all of my heart and I know that she loved me just as much. I can distinctly remember how Bootsie would see me on the other side of the yard, come over to me and rub her neck against my leg. This was her way of saying: "I need some attention". I would then scratch her head between her ears and scratch her back after which she was satisfied and would go and sit down.

People need love more than dogs do and when it is not received there can be strange repercussions. When love is not present in a person's life some of the results can be:
- •Limited appreciation of others.
- •Inability to freely give love.
- •The development of focusing on one's self.
- •Limited experiential knowledge of love.
- •Lack of trust for others.

Psychologists teach that all people have a need for significance and security. In order to be psychologically healthy, people must feel significant and they must feel secure. If you observe the people around you, it is easy to see that they are struggling with these needs. When people talk loud and cut up in public, it is obvious that they are in need of attention. They would NEVER admit it and probably don't even realize it. When people feel insecure, they act strange and do strange things.

A wise young man seeks to understand himself and how he was nurtured because it will affect everything that he does in life. ANSWER THIS QUESTION: Have you been left to yourself as far as discipline goes? Did your mother or father go upside your head when you acted up or did they just talk and let you get away with whatever you wanted to do?

The rod and reproof give wisdom: but the child left to himself bringeth his mother to shame.
Proverbs 29:15

I know that this may sound cruel but it is not, believe me. All throughout our history, parents have gotten on the cases of their children with whatever means necessary to BREAK that mean rebellious spirit in their children. Society today says that we should not "whip" (as we used to say) our children. They even put a big word on it to make it sound even more terrible, "CORPORAL PUNISHMENT!" Please note that proper discipline, administered by a loving parent is not abuse. Please note the following passages.

He that spareth his rod hateth his son: but he that loveth him chasteneth him betimes.
Proverbs 13:24

This simply means that a man who hates his son will not discipline him. The man that loves his son will discipline him when he needs it. This instills in a young man a sense of consequences for his actions. When this is absent in young men, they fear nothing and as a result die early.

Foolishness is bound in the heart of a child; but the rod of correction shall drive it far from him.
Proverbs 22:15

Foolishness comes with childhood. Sometimes I think of the foolish things that I did as a child that I thought were funny. Just thinking about these things scare me now that I am grown. When I was a child, we lived on a hill and my dad told us not to roll tires down the hill. It was fun to roll tires down the hill but we did not realize the danger involved.

A tire rolling down the hill would have enough momentum to go through a house if it hit it. We didn't understand nor perceive the danger involved so we continued to roll tires down the hill. One day, dad caught us rolling tires down the hill and he almost killed us. After we recovered, we never touched a tire again and now that we are grown we agree with what dad said. A good spanking, or whipping, or whatever you call it, will not hurt you if it is done in love.

> *Withhold not correction from the child: for if thou beatest him with the rod, he shall not die. Thou shalt beat him with the rod, and shalt deliver his soul from hell.*
>
> *Proverbs 23:13-14*

I must mention the fact that unfortunately many parents have taken the Biblical concept of discipline and abused it. Anytime you are spanked, or whipped for unclear reasons or because your parents were in a bad mood, is an unhealthy situation. Abuse could be defined as punishment administered without love. If you are a victim of excessive punishment there are some things that you must remember:

- God loves you and did not initiate the abuse.
- You must filter any negative feelings about the parent or adult that abused you so that you will be free from hatred and bitterness.
- Resolve to stop the abuse with your generation. Talk about your abuse to your wife and ask her to help you to release any frustration before you have children so that you will not repeat the abuse.

QUESTIONS
FOR INTROSPECTION AND DISCUSSION
(to make you think)

1. Tell the truth, shame the devil! Have you been disciplined enough by your parents? Are you able to get away with MURDER?

   _____

2. What makes you feel significant or important?_____

   _____

3. What makes you feel secure or safe?_____

4. Are you aware of any areas where you have not been properly nurtured?___Yes___No   If so, what are you doing about it? _____

5. What one thing did your parent(s) do to make you feel nurtured or loved?_____

APPLICABLE SCRIPTURES

> *For I was my father's son, tender and only beloved in the sight of my mother. He taught me also, and said unto me, Let thine heart retain my words: keep my commandments, and live.*
>
> *Proverbs 4:3,4*

> *The rod and reproof give wisdom: but a child left to himself bringeth his mother to shame.*
>
> *Proverbs 29:15*

Hatred stirreth up strifes: but love covereth all sins.
Proverbs 10:12

A friend loveth at all times, and a brother is born for adversity.
Proverbs 17:17

Notes:_____

_____

_____

_____

_____

_____

_____

_____

_____

_____

_____

CHAPTER THREE

Brothers And Sisters (Siblings)

I T TAKES MANY YEARS TO UNDERSTAND HOW your relationship with your brothers and sisters affects you. There are many adults in their forties who are just beginning to understand how the problems they had with their brothers and sisters while young have affected them all of these years. We could say that they have unresolved **sibling rivalries.** It is quite normal for there to be tension between children in the same home and when children fuss and fight it is a normal part of growing up. The problem comes when you have adults in their forties and fifties who are holding things against each other because of something that happened many years ago. This is an unhealthy situation.

If you have brothers and sisters, you should study your relationships to make sure that they are healthy. Here are some things to consider when dealing with your brothers and sisters.

1. THEY ARE HUMAN AND WILL MAKE MISTAKES

Ignorance means that you are not knowledgeable of a particular fact. It can also be used in the area of relationships by saying that he was ignorant of how she felt. People can be ignorant of others and unintentionally harm them. While growing up, brothers and sisters do things that hurt each other such as giving each other nicknames that scar us. It is possible to play a trick on a brother or sister that you feel is funny but they remember it painfully for many years. These

things are usually done in ignorance and we should consider them childhood mistakes.

2. IN A MOMENT OF WEAKNESS THEY MAY SAY OR DO SOMETHING THAT WILL HURT YOU.

Everybody has a bad day, a weak moment, a time when they will step on the neck of a loved one just to save their own skin. Brothers and sisters do this all of the time. Usually, they will realize that they were wrong and apologize either audibly, through gestures or some other way. Some people say they are sorry without saying that they are sorry. Don't hold this against them forever. Ask God to help you forgive them.

3. IF YOU FEEL THAT YOUR PARENTS TREAT THEM BETTER THAN THEY TREAT YOU, SEEK TO FIND OUT WHY.

Good parents know their children and deal with them according to their own personalities. Children don't usually understand this and will feel that the parents are choosing one child over the other. One child can handle money so he gets money; the other child can't handle money and blows it, so he gets less money. One daughter knows how to come in when she is supposed to, so she gets to go out, the other daughter does not know how to come in so she does not go out as much. There is generally a reason why parents treat one child differently from the other. Seek to find out why by observing the larger picture and listening when your parents give their responses to your requests.

4. IF YOUR PARENTS ACTUALLY DO TREAT YOUR BROTHER(S) OR SISTER(S) BETTER THAN THEY TREAT YOU, BE PATIENT.

I would like to come to your house, take you by the arm, go to a room which gives us privacy, look you dead in the eye and yell at the top of my lungs: "YOUR PARENTS AREN'T GOING TO DO EVERYTHING RIGHT, THEY

WILL MAKE MISTAKES!!!" Now, I admit that this is no excuse for the injustice that you will suffer, but the fact of the matter is that some parents prefer one child over another. In a dysfunctional family, there can be many reasons for this:

- One child is more appealing than the other.
- One child reminds a parent of the other parent which displeases the parent.
- The parent may fail to see the natural beauty in the child.
- Younger siblings benefit because the parents may have more money now than they did when you were young.

5. DON'T BE JEALOUS OF YOUR BROTHER'S OR SISTER'S SUCCESSES.

When you are jealous of others you are not focusing on your own God given strengths. This jealousy will cripple you as you attempt to succeed in life.

6. LEARN TO TALK OBJECTIVELY (with an open mind) WITH YOUR BROTHERS AND SISTERS ABOUT THE HURTS THAT THE TWO OF YOU HAVE SUFFERED WHILE GROWING UP.

The worse thing that you can do is to hold in the fact that your brother *&%#@ you off because he broke your bicycle when you were in the fifth grade and never said he was sorry and didn't even pay for it. Sit your brother or sister down and say: "We need to talk."

7. BE SURE TO FORGIVE THEM.

Forgiveness equals freedom for the one who forgives. To forgive is to free YOURSELF. Satan wants to bind you with the hurts of the past. Refuse to be enslaved to negative childhood memories. Set yourself free by forgiving those who have offended you. If you don't feel that you can face the person who hurt you then write a letter and send it to them. If the person is dead then pull up a chair and talk to the chair. The point to remember is that you have to get it out. This is where healing begins.

8. SEE TO IT THAT THE MISTAKES OF THE PAST ARE NOT REPEATED.

We should all take personal responsibility in seeing to it that we don't repeat the mistakes our parents made with us. We should also seek to limit the damage caused by mistakes and scars between our brothers and sisters. One thing I am doing with my children is, I am going to see to it that they study, participate in class and get their homework done even if I have to live at the school. I am sure you have some things that you would like to do differently when you have kids.

Seek to develop a better relationship with your brother(s) and sister(s). If they won't act right, you keep on loving them and seeking to develop a relationship with them and God will do the rest. If you are reading this book, God is trying to give you what you need to repair any broken relationships.

QUESTIONS
FOR INTROSPECTION AND DISCUSSION
(to make you think)

1. Do you have any brothers? ___Yes___No
   If so, how many? _____

2. Do you have any sisters? ___Yes___No
   If so, how many?_____

3. Have they ever hurt you? ___Yes___No
   If so, how?_____

4. How do you see yourself rating in the family?
   ___favorite   ___average   ___least favorite

5. What coping skills did you develop to deal with your
   position in the family?_____

6. Do you understand why your parents treat you the way they
   do?   ___Yes___No

7. Can you talk to your brother/sister about the things in your
   family that hurt you and you don't understand?
   ___Yes___No

8. Have you forgiven your brother/sister/parents for how they
   hurt you? ___Yes___No

9. Name or list three things that happened to you that you
   don't want to happen to your kids.
   1._____
   2._____
   3._____

10. Do you need to call a brother/sister and settle some things
    with them?   ___Yes___No

APPLICABLE SCRIPTURES

> *A brother offended is harder to be won than a strong city: and their contentions are like the bars of a castle.*
>
> *Proverbs 18:19*

> *A man that hath friends must show himself friendly: and there is a friend that sticketh closer than a brother.*
>
> *Proverbs 18:24*

> *And when his brethren saw that their father loved him more than all his brethren, they hated him, and could not speak peaceably unto him.*
>
> *Genesis 37:4*

> *And Isaac loved Esau, because he did eat of his venison: but Rebekah loved Jacob.*
>
> *Genesis 25:28*

> *A friend loveth at all times, and a brother is born for adversity.*
>
> *Proverbs 17:17*

> *Then came Peter to him, and saith, Lord, how oft shall my brother sin against me, and I forgive him: till seven times? Jesus saith unto him, I say not unto thee, Until seven times: but, Until seventy times seven.*
>
> *Matthew 18:21-22*

CHAPTER FOUR

Living In The Projects, A Housing Development (or living in the trap of a poor hood)

RECENTLY I WAS SPENDING SOME TIME IN A housing project in our city. As a grown man, I am fascinated with the projects because I lived in one as a child. I now spend time there seeking to enrich the lives of children who live there. When I lived there as a child, I learned how to be amused with whatever was lying around. I made toys out of trash and entertained myself with whatever I found.

The other day while in the neighborhood I found myself doing something that I had done as a child. I was looking at the ground. While looking at the ground, I found a quarter on the street and a cat's-eye marble partly submerged in the dirt outside of an apartment. I was excited with my discovery and I found myself reliving part of my childhood. Even though I am many years removed from the "manor" as we use to call it, the "manor" is still very much in me. I have a fondness for the atmosphere that is found there. Even the negative aspects of the projects are firmly a part of my past that I think of occasionally.

If you are a young man who was raised or is being raised in the projects there are some things that I learned as I grew up that you should be aware of now.

1. YOU CAN WORK YOUR WAY OUT OF THE PROJECTS.

We know about sports as a way out, but we need to consider some additional ways that are less based on chance.

•Education will get you out of the projects, and it will enrich your personal life.

•The Army will get you out of the projects, but without the education you may end up right back.

•Musical talent may get you out of the projects, but without an education you may end up right back.

•There are many illegal ways to get out of the projects, but you may die or go to jail in the process.

My wife and I made it out of the projects and out of poverty through education. With an education you have a better chance of getting a job and the education helps you better understand the world in which you live.

2. TURN ANY ANGER INTO POSITIVE ENERGY.

I used to watch my dad clean toilets with his hands and it made me angry because racism limited him to that job. I grabbed that anger, refused to throw bricks during the riots but took that energy and channeled it into building my own business and getting an education.

Look around you. Does what you see (drugs, crime, despair, poverty) make you angry? If it does, good! Take the energy that results from that anger and channel it into those things (education, integrity, love, prayer, work) that will make a difference. NEVER WASTE YOUR ANGER! Seek to develop the habit of directing the energy that comes from your anger in positive ways.

3. REFUSE TO BE APATHETIC.

Apathy is when you just don't care. Many people die in projects in poverty because they became apathetic (ain't no use tryin', they ain't gonna let us get no where). Say to yourself "I can do all things through Christ who strengthens me" and I can work my way out of here.

Black folks created the blues and we could sing them because we were oppressed. I feel that the blues as an art form is an important part of our history which should be maintained. On the other hand, singing the blues will not help you elevate your thinking to where it should be maintained. Learn to cultivate a passion toward improving your status in life. Don't hang around negative, lazy, apathetic people who are going no where.

4. DON'T BE STINGY

Learn to become a flowing brook and not a stagnant pond. Water flows in and out of a brook and it stays fresh. Water flows into a pond, stays there and gets stale.

> *The liberal soul shall be made fat: and he that waterth shall be watered also himself.*
> *Proverbs 11:25*

Learn to give and be sure not to step on people as you rise out of poverty. When you step on people to get ahead you will find yourself standing on shaky ground.

> *Give, and it shall be given unto you; good measure, pressed down, and shaken together, and running over, shall men give into your bosom. For with the same measure that you mete withal it shall be measured to you again.*
> *Luke 6:38*

I am sure that you have heard people say: "You reap what you sow." This simply means what you dish out will come back to you. This applies to the good as well as to the bad.

5. DEVELOP AN EMPOWERMENT MENTALITY NOW.

Just because you live in the ghetto does not mean that you need to have a ghetto mind set. When you open your mouth, people should not be able to tell what part of town you are from. No one can imprison your mind. 'Kunta Kinte' was a slave in body but never in his mind. Our problem today is many men are slaves in their minds which also puts their bodies into slavery.

6. DETERMINE TO ONLY OPEN YOUR MOUTH WITH WISDOM OR KEEP IT SHUT.

Some people talk too soon, too loud, too fast, too much and about nothin'. James Brown had a popular song a few years ago titled "Talkin' Loud and Sayin' Nothin'."

> *Even a fool, when he holdeth his peace, is counted*
> *wise: and he that shutteth his lips is esteemed a man*
> *of understanding.*
> *Proverbs 17:28*

There is a time to be quiet and there is a time to display wisdom.

> *Pleasant words are as an honeycomb, sweet to the*
> *soul, and health to the bones.*
> *Proverbs 16:24*

When people observe your wisdom, discernment and discretion they will pay attention. Webster defines wisdom as the quality of being wise or the power of judging rightly and following the soundest course of action, based on knowledge, experience, understanding, etc. Discernment is defined as the power of discerning; keen perception or judgment; insight; acumen. Discretion is defined as: the freedom or authority to make decisions and choices; power to judge or act.

Your gift of wisdom will work on your behalf if you let the right people see it.

> *A man's gift maketh room for him, and bringeth him before great men.*
>
> *Proverbs 18:16*

Strive to develop the gift of wisdom which will help guide you as you seek to make money off of your other gifts. We all know of many young, gifted Black men who were destroyed because they did not have the wisdom to handle success and the money that came with it.

> *Wisdom is the principle thing; therefore get wisdom: and with all thy getting get understanding.*
>
> *Proverbs 4:7*

7. RESOLVE TO TAKE EVERY OPPORTUNITY TO HELP OTHERS BETTER THEMSELVES.

There is a rich, gratifying sense of accomplishment you get when you help others. When you help others, you are planting seeds in your flower garden that will one day bloom and bless you. There is a law or principle that you employ when you help others. It is the principle of reaping and sowing. The fact that you reap what you sow can work to your own good if you sow good things.

So, where do you live? If you live in the projects it is possible to move out right now simply by changing your thinking. If you don't take the time and effort to learn how to lift your thinking to a higher plane, it is possible that you will never leave the projects. In order to escape poverty, you must first enrich your mind.

QUESTIONS
FOR INTROSPECTION AND DISCUSSION
(to make you think)

1. Have you ever lived in the projects in or poverty?
   Yes___ No___

2. If so, how long? _____

3. What were your plans for getting out of the situation?
   _____

4. What steps have you already taken toward that goal? (write or discuss them) _____
   _____

5. Who have you discussed your plans with and allowed to evaluate them? _____

6. Of the seven suggestions given in this chapter to help you out of the hood, which do you need to work on?

   _____

   _____

APPLICABLE SCRIPTURES

Wisdom is the principal thing; therefore get wisdom: and with all thy getting get understanding
                                    Proverbs 4:7

Trust in the LORD with all thine heart; and lean not unto thine own understanding.   In all thy ways acknowledge him, and he shall direct thy paths.
                                    Proverbs 3:5-6

Give, and it shall be given unto you; good measure, pressed down, and shaken together, and running over, shall men give into your bosom.   For with the same measure that ye mete withal it shall be measured to you again.
                                    Luke 6:38

I can do all things through Christ which strengtheneth me.
                                    Philippians 4:13

CHAPTER FIVE

Blocks
(Our Fears And Anxieties That Stop Us In Life)

IN THE SUMMER OF MY SIXTH YEAR OF LIVE MY family moved from a house to a large public housing complex (the projects). The first day there I was pleased and surprised when a group of kids came to my front door and asked my mom if I could come out and play. She responded positively and I soon found myself outside with a group of young people playing and having big fun. All of a sudden without any warning, the kids stopped playing and I found myself in the middle of a circle that they had made around me. The leader of the group was a kid named Mikey. He walked up to me, grabbed me by the collar and said: "I heard that you think you are baad"?!!, to which I quickly replied: "Who told you that?, I never said that I was bad." At that point he let me go and everyone returned back to their fun and games.

I had learned an important lesson about my new neighborhood. If I was to have any clout in the neighborhood, I would have to work my way up the ladder, one kid at a time. As time passed, I found out that Carl was no problem because he was a crybaby. BoBo was big, but he was slow and I learned to hit him several times real fast and the fight was over. But there was a problem when it came to Mikey. I had what is called a mental block when it came to Mikey. This mental block led me to believe that I would never be able to overcome his meanness and power.

Mikey did a good job of making a lasting first impression when I was most vulnerable. When we are vulnerable we remember events very well that in a different setting would not bother us. Mikey, in my face on my first day in the hood, is stamped on my memory for the rest of my life. I firmly believe that if Carl or BoBo would have gotten to me on that first day, I would not have been able to beat them and move up in rank. **The fact that I had the opportunity to study them without fear allowed me to accurately assess their strengths and weaknesses and challenge them with confidence.**

I must say that I never beat Mikey. I never got up enough nerve to overcome the mental damage that he did to me on my first day in the hood. Now that I am grown, I understand that **I HAD A MENTAL BLOCK.**

THE DAWNING OF BLOCKS

Blocks are most dangerous during the formative years (childhood). This is why it is so important for little children to be treated fairly. When I was in the first grade a White kid hit me in the nose and it hurt. I can remember going to the White teacher and through tears telling her what happened. Her response was: "shut up and get in line." As a first grader, I immediately determined that several things were true:

- This White woman did not care about my nose.
- If this thing called education, which to me meant getting fair treatment from this White woman, is going to be so painful, I DON'T NEED IT!
- I had better protect myself and keep my mouth shut. Therefore while in class, I'll be quiet, but on the playground while the White teacher ain't lookin', I will rule the class.

Blocks that occur during the formative years (while you are growing up) do an extensive amount of damage. They are bad because children don't understand the danger in

44

not talking about those painful events so that they can heal from them.

THE DANGER OF BLOCKS

We can clearly see how blocks can cause a person to **FOREGO OPPORTUNITIES.** I personally feel that the damage I received while in the first grade caused me to miss many opportunities for academic advancement. It was not until I was older and understood what happened that I was able to heal myself and reteach myself. In my mind, I became the teacher and punished the child that hit me in the nose. Blocks will also make you **FOCUS ON FAILURE.** A block usually positions itself at a very busy intersection in your brain. It does this so that all of your positive thoughts will have to pass by MR. BLOCK. When the positive thoughts pass by MR. BLOCK, he reminds them that it is rough out there and you probably won't make it. Our blocks are one of the reasons we focus our attention on past failures.

THE DESIRE OF BLOCKS

Blocks are **TOOLS OF TERRORISTS.** When people purposely or accidently scar you, it is similar to a terrorist attack. The reason is that damage is not always immediately apparent, and it can be difficult to properly place the blame.

Blocks are also **TACTICS OF THE TORMENTOR.** Satan wants to ruin us all while we are young. If he can get us while we are young, he has us for a lifetime. Satan has servants (child molesters, mean adults, mean kids) whose job it is to place a scar on young minds so that they will grow in a dysfunctional way.

THE DEMISE OF BLOCKS

I am glad to report that we need not be controlled by

our damage, scars or blocks. God is there to help us overcome them. Here is how you can destroy the blocks in your life.

> •**Solicit the help of the Holy Spirit.** He is the one who helps us identify the blocks we picked up early in our lives. He will give you strength as you face those frightening scars of the past.

> •**Make satan fight fairly.** Satan fights us everyday. We must learn to detect illegal blows (below the belt) and make sure we get points for satan's illegal blows. Well, the question on the floor is: "What is an illegal blow by satan?" The answer is, anytime satan tortures you with a failure from your past, it is an illegal blow. When this happens you must say: "THAT AIN'T FAIR!!, THAT DIDN'T COUNT!!"

When satan tempts us to feel guilty about something that happened in the past, we should refuse to participate. It is spiritually illegal to feel guilty about something in the past that you can't change. We do need to feel guilty about it initially and then recover and move on. Don't fight satan's illegal battles, do fight his legal battles. There are temptations and battles that we do need to fight and cry about. Those are the battles that we can do something about. When satan tempts us right now, the bell has rung and the fight has begun. Please note that this is a fair fight. We must trust Christ to sustain us when we are tempted with the legal stuff and the decision has to be made right then to do right.

THE DAWNING OF FREEDOM
Once you develop the art of consciously and actively

identifying, confronting, and dealing with the scars and blocks in your life you have developed a skill that will help you be free to reach your full potential. You can now become successful personally and professionally. More importantly, with your new found freedom, you can really like yourself.

QUESTIONS
FOR INTROSPECTION OR DISCUSSION
(to make you think)

1. What personal blocks are you aware of?_____

_____

2. Have you analyzed how they paralyze you?_____

3. Are you prepared to deal with them or are you afraid to face them right now?_____

4. Discuss with a mature friend how your personal blocks have stunted your growth. Discuss what steps you can take to overcome your blocks.

5. What one thing makes you feel guilty or ashamed?_____

6. Have you figured out if this is something you should feel guilty about?_____

APPLICABLE SCRIPTURES

> *And I will restore to you the years that the locust hath eaten, the cankerworm, and the caterpillar, and the palmerworm, my great army which I sent among you.*
> *Joel 2:25*

I can do all things through Christ which strengtheneth me.

Philippians 4:13

Likewise the Spirit also helpeth our infirmities: for we know not what we should pray for as we ought: but the Spirit itself maketh intercession for us with groanings which cannot be uttered.

Romans 8:26

Submit yourselves therefore to God. Resist the devil, and he will flee from you.

James 4:7

Ye are of God, little children, and have overcome them: because greater is he that is in you, than he that is in the world.

I John 4:4

For God hath not given us the spirit of fear; but of power, and of love, and of a sound mind.

II Timothy 1:7

No weapon that is formed against thee shall prosper; and every tongue that shall rise against thee in judgment thou shalt condemn. This is the heritage of the servants of the Lord, and their righteousness is of me, saith the Lord.

Isaiah 54:17

PART TWO

NO WEAPON FORMED AGAINST ME SHALL PROSPER

CHAPTER SIX

What Kind Of Gang
Are You In?

T HE HUMAN BEING IS A COMMUNAL creature. In other words, we all like to have friends and associates. Young people are especially prone to feel that they need a friend or a click to hang with. While all of this is natural and good, it can be taken to extremes.

The term "Gang" carries with it the image of coercion, aggressive persuasion, violence and the reckless following of a misguided leader. Many young people who get involved in gangs make the mistake of going to the wrong people for support. There are a multitude of reasons people get involved in gangs but none of the reasons can be justified when you consider the end result of much of the gang activity we see in society today.

Actually there are associations that are established and accepted by society. We do not call them gangs but they all meet the same fundamental need that a gang meets. Some of these organizations are called "tribes, teams, clans, races, fraternities, sororities, and clubs." These organizations meet the need of providing a feeling of safety and giving credibility to one's existence.

Things you should consider when you are tempted to become involved in a gang:

1. ASK YOURSELF THE QUESTION: "WHY DO I NEED TO BE INVOLVED?"

If you have glaring unmet needs, it is easy to believe

that those needs can be met through gang activity. Anytime you are drawn to a group of people or an individual you should seek to know why you are drawn in that direction.

2. WHAT IS IT THAT THE GANG WILL SUPPLY THAT I CANNOT GET IN OTHER PLACES?

Many young people find love, acceptance and a sense of belonging in a gang. I would like to submit that these fundamental needs can be found in other places. There is a principle that comes from this Scripture that tells us how to get friends.

> *A man that hath friends must show himself friendly: and there is a friend that sticketh closer than a brother.*
>
> *Proverbs 18:24*

It is a fact that if you need friends the only way to get them is to be friendly. I challenge you to initiate friendship by showing yourself friendly. I have many friends and the reason that I have them is that I am a very friendly person. I have cultivated the ability to go into a room of complete strangers and strike up a conversation, make them feel at ease and comfortable with me. With this ability I am never alone very long because people flock to kind, friendly persons.

3. CONSIDER THE LONG TERM CONSEQUENCES OF YOUR INVOLVEMENT.

Can you name three persons who were deeply involved in gangs and somehow got out of the gangs and lived happily ever after? The odds are against you naming three people. If you can name three people who are doing well, I am sure that you are aware that they were negatively impacted by their gang involvement. One of the greatest talents that a young man can develop is the ability to look at another's mistakes and learn from them. One of the perils of being young is that you have this false belief that somehow you will not get caught and that you will be successful doing something that you have seen others fail at. "Yea, I'm not going to get caught, I'm too smooth." These are popular last words of many foolish young men.

4. CONSIDER HOW YOUR OTHER FAMILY MEMBERS WILL BE IMPACTED BY YOUR INVOLVEMENT.

One of the terrible consequences of gang involvement is that your family will be affected. We all have heard of situations in which ruthless gang members have attacked innocent women and children because of a disagreement they had with another gang member. There is a saying that goes like this: There is no honor among thieves. The Scripture says it like this:

> *But evil men and seducers shall wax worse and worse, deceiving, and being deceived.*
>
> *II Timothy 3:13*

This Scripture states that evil men and those who seduce others will get worse and worse as time passes. It also goes on to state that they will deceive or run games on others and they will be deceived in the end. So, God says that if you deceive others, all you are doing is assuring that in the future you will be deceived. There is no escaping this principle or law! So, no matter how nice the gang members appear to be, there will be a deterioration in the relationship as time passes and your family may be sucked into the confusion.

5. ASK YOURSELF THE QUESTION: "HOW WILL

GANG INVOLVEMENT RESTRICT MY THINKING?"

One characteristic of gang activity is that it restricts individuality. You must think like the gang and put the interests and mindset of the gang first. You must hate whom they hate and love whom they love. It is a fact that you will become like the people that you hang with. You may deny this all you want to but the facts are in. I had an older dope addict tell me that: "You can't hang with the coolie boys and don't do dope." The Scripture says it this way:

> *Be not deceived: evil communications corrupt good manners.*
>
> *I Corinthians 15:33*

Before you join a gang consider the mindset of those in the gang and ask yourself the question: "Do I want to think like they think?"

6. IF YOU ARE BEING FORCED TO JOIN A GANG, WHAT ALTERNATIVES DO YOU FEEL YOU HAVE?

    a. Move (a forced relocation)

    b. Resist involvement

    c. Join a local Church

    d. _____

The pressure placed on young people to join a gang can be immense. I feel that one of the first things you should do when this happens is to consult with an older wiser person. If you don't do this, you may make the wrong decision under pressure. Consider having a pastor, police officer, teacher or relative assist you.

QUESTIONS
FOR INTROSPECTION AND DISCUSSION
(to make you think)

1. Have you been pressured to join a gang? Yes____ No____

2. Do you have friends who are in gangs? Yes___ No___

3. Is your self-esteem high enough that you don't need to join a gang? Yes___ No___

4. Do you live in a gang-infested area? Yes___ No___

5. What do you feel are the best defenses against gang activity?

_____

6. How do you feel the home life affects gang involvement?

_____

_____

7. On the positive side, what groups are you involved in that provide many of the things that a gang provides but without the negatives of gang association?_____

8. What suggestions would you have for the younger brother regarding gangs. _____

APPLICABLE SCRIPTURES

My son, if sinners entice thee, consent thou not. If they say, Come with us, let us lay wait for blood, let us lurk privily for the innocent without cause: let us swallow them up alive as the grave; and whole, as those that go down into the pit: We shall find all precious substance, we shall fill our houses with spoil: Cast in thy lot among us; let us all have one purse: My son, walk not thou in the way with them; refrain thy foot from their path: For their feet run to evil, and make haste to shed blood.
Proverbs 1:10-16

Discretion shall preserve thee, understanding shall keep thee: To deliver thee from the way of the evil man, from the man that speaketh froward things;
Proverbs 2:11-12

Trust in the LORD with all thine heart; and lean not unto thine own understanding. In all thy ways acknowledge him, and he shall direct thy paths.
Proverbs 3:5-6

Happy is the man that findeth wisdom, and the man that getteth understanding.
Proverbs 3:13

Strive not with a man without cause, if he have done thee no harm.
Proverbs 3:30

Enter not into the path of the wicked, and go not in the way of evil men. Avoid it, pass not by it, turn from it, and pass away. For they sleep not, except they have done mischief; and their sleep is taken away, unless they cause some to fall. For they eat the bread of wickedness, and drink the wine of violence. But the path of the just is as the shining light, that shineth more and more unto the perfect day. The way of the wicked is as darkness: they know not at what they stumble.

Proverbs 4:14-19

Notes:_____

_____

_____

_____

_____

_____

_____

_____

_____

_____

_____

_____

_____

_____

_____

_____

_____

CHAPTER SEVEN

How Does Your Size Affect You?
(Endomorph- Ectomorph - Mesomorph)

I HAD JUST PASSED TO THE 7TH GRADE AND MY family moved from the west side to what we called the up town area of my city. All of my life I had lived on the west side and at this critical period in my development, we moved. It was very difficult because I had to start all over making new friends on a new side of town. On one particular day I rode my bicycle through the neighborhood hoping to find a friend. I came across some people my age sitting on the loading dock of a paper company. As I pulled up on my bike, I noticed that they were ratting each other or playing the dozens. This was quite amusing until an older, bigger guy named Kenny looked at me and said: "What you laughing at?, You need to go home and jump out of those dingaling pants!" (my pants were hand-me-downs from my older brother). I quickly came back and told him that: " I <u>CAN</u> go home and jump out of these dingaling pants but you <u>CAN'T</u> go home and jump out of those dingaling lips." Everybody laughed and I had obviously scored a significant point. The only bad part was that Kenny got mad. Now, Kenny was too big and old to jump on me, but there was a guy there who could, named Magoo.

They called him Magoo because he was big for his age and goofy. Kenny said to Magoo: "Hey Magoo, I bet you can't beat him" (talking about me). To this Magoo replied: "Yes I can," Kenny said: "No you can't," to which Magoo said: "Yes I can," and in a matter of seconds I was in a fight with a goofy FAT dude. I felt like I didn't have a friend in the world. There I was a skinny dude in a fight with a fat dude which was started by an older muscular dude.

Size is very important when you are young. It is also very important to learn how to capitalize on the size that God gave you and use it to your best advantage. Endomorph, Ectomorph, Mesomorph, respectively, are the technical names for fat, skinny and muscular body types. Whether or not you know it or want to acknowledge it, your body type has a lot to do with how you view yourself and how others view you. The goal of this chapter is to help you consider your attitude about your body size and help you determine what attitudinal adjustments you need to make in order to have a healthy self-esteem. Also, we want to examine how others, (teachers, White police officers, store clerks, etc.) relate to your body size.

LET'S CONSIDER THE ENDOMORPH (Fat Dudes)

Not too long ago, I was visiting with a youth group. There was a young man in the group who was very large. He was an endomorph, or we would say fat. To my amazement this brother was much younger than I thought he was. He appeared to be High School age, but he was only in elementary school.

It is a fact that young people are eating more today than they did in years past and it is also a fact that the fast foods are high in fat content. For this and other reasons, there are many young men who are large for their age. If you are a large young man, and have an endomorphic body type, you need to analyze how it has affected you. Is your self-esteem in tact? Have you taken the time to analyze why you are big? Is it in your genes or do you just eat a lot?

Sometimes young men will eat when they are depressed, feel defeated, helpless and hopeless. Friction in the home can lead young men to eat as a way to escape. When we add to that the various video games which tend to limit exercise, we see why the rate of obesity is increasing.

I WANT TO CHALLENGE THE ENDOMORPH TO DO SEVERAL THINGS:

1. MAKE SURE THAT YOU ARE GETTING ENOUGH EXERCISE.

As you get older this need will become more apparent.

2. DEVELOP A DISCIPLINE REGARDING YOUR EATING HABITS.

Don't eat late at night. Try to eat healthy foods (fruits, vegetables, etc.). If you do this you will thank yourself for it later.

3. DETERMINE NOT TO BE DEFEATED BY A WEIGHT PROBLEM.

Never give up. Remember that everyone is struggling with some real or imagined deficiency. Some deficiencies are more visible than others. Remember that your problem is common and God can help you get over it.

4. DECIDE WHERE YOU WANT TO EXCEL IN LIFE AND PURSUE EXCELLENCE WITH ALL OF YOUR MIGHT.

You must believe that you are gifted and good at something. Seek to find what that is and get even better at it. I grew up with a friend who had a physical deformity. His hobby was collecting model airplanes. While other kids were out playing he would be inside studying the various types of planes. He learned so much with his childhood hobby that he was able to get a job as an adult with an aerospace company.

5. IF YOU ARE REALLY BOTHERED BY YOUR WEIGHT, SEEK OUT SOMEONE YOU CAN TALK TO ABOUT IT.

This will help you overcome the mental blocks about your weight. Some have overcome the anxiety regarding their weight and others have learned how to manage their weight.

6. STRIVE TO BREAK THE STANDARD STEREOTYPES REGARDING FAT PEOPLE BY BEING NEAT, WELL GROOMED, AND A HARD WORKER.

When you conform to the negative stereotypes people see you as one who is molded by his situation or controlled by others.

7. IF YOU NEED HELP, GO TO AN ADULT AND OPENLY EXPRESS YOUR CONCERN TO THEM AND ASK THEM FOR HELP.

If they don't help you, go to another adult. I know of a child that used to worry me to death about her needs. I did not always have the time or cash to help her but I appreciated her gumption, zeal, nerve, aggression and goal oriented personality. She knew that I wanted her to succeed in life and she challenged me to help her.

Remember, Your Size Will Not Cause You To Fail In Life, But Your Attitude About Your Size Could Be your Downfall!!

The endomorph should consider how others view fat Black young men. Consider these facts:

• You look older than you are. Remember that older people aren't exactly sure how to treat you.

• Strive to make your behavior match your perceived age. For example, if you are 12 years old and you look 15, act more mature when in the presence of strangers.

• Remember that if you act aggressive or violent that you will be dealt with as an adult. People are generally afraid of you so be sure not to give any indication that you are violent.

LET'S CONSIDER THE ECTOMORPH (Little Dudes)

Ectomorphs are little dudes. Little dudes have a totally different set of problems than fat dudes. I have a little friend who is an ectomorph. As I have observed him over the years, I have learned some interesting things about ectomorphs from my little friend. I also know a lot from experience because I was an ectomorph as a young man.

Ectomorphs must be careful not to work hard just so that others will accept them. It is characteristic of little dudes to try to overcompensate for their size. It seems like they are always trying to prove something. Little dudes have been known to have limited patience. When threatened, they will go on the offensive very quickly.

In some cases, ectomorphs retreat from sports and physical activity to the academic arena. The stereotypical 90lb. weakling who makes straight "A's" is generally an ectomorph. He is the one that the girls look at last and he may struggle to get a date. Please note that these are just stereotypes and don't have to be true if you are an ectomorph.

I WANT TO CHALLENGE THE ECTOMORPH TO DO SEVERAL THINGS:

1. TAKE TIME TO STOP AND CONSIDER ANY FEELINGS OF INFERIORITY YOU HAVE WHEN YOU ARE AROUND BIGGER GUYS.

You will never reach your full potential if your path is lined by negative thoughts regarding those who are bigger than you are.

2. WORK TO DEVELOP THE ATTITUDE THAT YOUR SIZE IS A UNIQUE ASSET AS OPPOSED TO A LIABILITY.

You should view life like you view basketball. What I mean is that because of my size, there are some positions on the court that I do not play well. On one occasion while playing basketball, I found myself in the hole (under the basket) with the big men. I saw the ball coming down and I jumped up to get it. The only problem is that the big men (some weighing 100lbs more than I do) saw the ball also and they jumped to get it also. At that moment I realized that I was not playing the game wisely. So, I moved outside and started working on my killer jump shot while using my speed to out maneuver the big dudes.

3. MAKE A LIST OF THE MANY THINGS THAT YOU CAN DO WELL.

To focus on the positive gifts and abilities that you have is a healthy habit. It helps you see the positive side of your existence rather than focusing on what you can't do. You should take the time to write your strengths down on a sheet of paper. Writing these things down will further enhance your understanding and awareness of the areas in which you are strong.

4. DON'T BE AFRAID TO BE SMART.

Anyone who does not appreciate your God-given brains is either jealous or is not your friend. In either case you should not concern yourself with how they feel about you. I know kids who are so insecure about themselves that they will purposely not do their best in order to fit in with some of the kids who put pressure on them.

5. BE SENSITIVE TO THE TEMPTATION TO OVERCOMPENSATE FOR YOUR SIZE BY DOING THINGS SUCH AS HAVING THREE GIRLFRIENDS, DRESSING CRAZY OR ANY SUCH THING.

To **overcompensate** for your size is to say to the world: "I don't like myself or I'm not satisfied with myself". People can see how you are behaving and will believe that you have a weak personality. Resist the temptation to overcompensate for your size. Please, always do your best, but don't overcompensate.

The small dude needs to consider how others view him. Generally ectomorphs are seen as less of a threat than endomorphs or mesomorphs. It is advisable for the small dude to have a healthy vocabulary and learn how to use it wisely. Ectomorphs have a tendency to run their mouths. Try to control that temptation and attempt to speak with wisdom. This can help you gain the respect that you may not otherwise get. It is possible for ectomorphs to gain access to positions and opportunities that others may not get because of the fact that they are not physically threatening. Be sure to take advantage of this.

LET'S LOOK AT THE MESOMORPH
(Muscular Dudes)

The mesomorph is the muscular type. I live in a

college town and there are a lot of athletes in this town. I frequently watch the University of Illinois football and basketball teams on television to see how the season is going. Not long ago, I was in the grocery store when a van load of athletes came into the store. At first I thought it was an invasion of giants. When they came in the store it was as if everybody else in the store shrank. Mesomorphs are imposing people.

I have a good friend who is muscular. One day while we were playing, I jumped on his back, wrapped my arms around him in an attempt to hold him. He simply exhaled, and lifted his arms, breaking my hold with little to no effort.

In our society people are impressed with muscular men. It has always been that way with human beings. I think of the children of Israel who when they wanted a king, looked on the physical stature of a man named Saul. The Bible says of Saul that from his shoulders up he was higher than any of the people. He was chosen to be the king when the people wanted a king. The interesting thing is that he did not make a good king. You see, a man must be a king on the inside before he can ever be a good king, regardless of what he looks like on the outside.

I WANT TO CHALLENGE THE MESOMORPH TO DO SEVERAL THINGS:

1. TAKE ADVANTAGE OF THE MYSTIQUE THAT COMES WITH HAVING A MESOMORPHIC BODY TYPE.

This mystique can help you get jobs and positions of leadership. There have been many studies done that show that the tall, dark, handsome men get the best jobs. I know that it is unfair but it is a fact of life that is a plus for the mesomorphs and causes others to work a little harder.

2. REMEMBER THAT AS YOU GET OLDER, THE MYSTIQUE AND ITS ADVANTAGES WILL DIMINISH.

As with Saul, the mystique wore off and the people were depending on his character, wisdom, integrity, and courage to lead them. Saul was lacking in these areas. Although others may be impressed with your size, don't you be impressed, instead prepare for your future when size is no longer an asset.

3. DON'T NEGLECT TO GET AN EDUCATION.

Once you and your admirers become adults, the fascination over your body will diminish and you will need to be qualified to get a job. This is particularly important with the young Black males who only want to be in the NFL or NBA. There is nothing sadder than a 6'3" Black male with no education who almost made it to the big money arena of professional sports. This brother's past great moments on the court are now forgotten because people will forget quickly. The only thing that can help him now is an education or a rich uncle.

4. DON'T ALLOW THE ATHLETIC COMMUNITY TO PUSH YOU IF YOU DON'T FEEL GIFTED IN THAT AREA.

Just because you are muscular does not mean that you should be an athlete. You will never be a great athlete unless your heart is in it. Another sad situation is the Black males who play sports and get hurt because they really weren't gifted athletes.

5. MAKE SURE THAT ANY WOMAN THAT YOU ARE WITH HAS CONSIDERED YOUR PERSONALITY AS WELL AS YOUR PHYSICAL ATTRACTION.

It is a fact that men want beautiful women and women want handsome men. This natural tendency can get you into big trouble in the long run. If she is only interested in you while the crowds are shouting and there is a chance for a professional career, then you are in trouble. You will be better off with a woman that you seek out rather than a woman who seeks you out. (I know I'm right about it.)

QUESTIONS
FOR INTROSPECTION AND DISCUSSION
(to make you think)

1. What is your body type?_____

2. What are you doing to take advantage of it?_____

3. Can you name a specific occasion when your body type came in handy? Explain_____

4. Can you name an occasion when your body type was a source of trouble? Explain_____

5. Have you considered the negatives of your body type?

_____

6. Have you talked to someone about any concerns you may have in this area?_____

APPLICABLE SCRIPTURES

The glory of young men is their strength: and the beauty of old men is the grey head.

Proverbs 20:29

Give not thy strength unto women, nor thy ways to that which destroyeth kings.

Proverbs 31:3

Then said I, Wisdom is better than strength:

Ecclesiastes 9:16a

And there we saw the giants, the sons of Anak, which come of the giants: and we were in our own sight as grasshoppers, and so we were in their sight.

Numbers 13:33

And Jesus increased in wisdom and stature, and in favor with God and man.

Luke 2:52

And he had a son, whose name was Saul, a choice young man, and a goodly: and there was not among the children of Israel a goodlier person than he: from his shoulders and upward he was higher than any of the people.

I Samuel 9:2

Notes:_____

_____

_____

_____

_____

_____

_____

_____

_____

_____

_____

_____

_____

_____

_____

_____

CHAPTER EIGHT

DRUGS
(The Contemporary Slavemaster)

WHEN A PERSON GETS HIGH, THAT PERson alters his state of consciousness. When young people drink alcohol, smoke pot or even do `cane, they are altering their state of consciousness. This is accomplished in many cases by decreasing the amount of oxygen that goes to the brain. For each drug, the body's function is altered in a manner in which the conscious state of the individual is altered. In many cases, people think this is fun and they will laugh and giggle while high, but in reality serious damage is being done to the body while in this state.

So, I would like to suggest to you today that when we consider the issue of drugs, we should look at ourselves and determine how do we handle reality. Do we seek to escape from our world and problems by any means? Here are some things to consider:

HOW HEALTHY IS YOUR PERSONAL ESTEEM?

A person's self-esteem will affect their need for crutches. I was always amazed by people that I grew up with who could look at temptation (drugs, women, money) in the eye and say: "I don't want any!" This would always blow my mind. In most cases, the reason a person can say this is that they know who they are and know what they want in life. Earlier chapters in this book have pointed out the need to really search to determine strengths and weaknesses so that we are aware of our areas of vulnerability.

HOW DO YOU COPE WITH PERSONAL PROBLEMS?

Problems can be devastating! The problems of youth only compound themselves in later life. One of the greatest gifts you can give yourself is the gift of studying and applying problem solving skills. No problem should be allowed to have a greater influence on you than it deserves. Many times it is our inappropriate response to a minor problem that creates a bigger problem. I have learned (as ridiculous as this sounds) to view each problem as an opportunity to grow, especially in the area of relationships.

HOW AGGRESSIVELY DO YOU SHUN DRUGS?

Just the other day, I was talking to a young man who had been on drugs for two years. He stated that it all started when he innocently went to a party. As the party progressed, the drugs were put on the table. He stated that he knew he should have left immediately. Unfortunately, he didn't leave and his life is currently in shambles as a result.

It is a wise man who walks away from drugs and any form of pressure from "friends" who would bring drugs into his presence. A simple point to remember is that anyone who would attempt to get you high is not a friend but a minister (servant) of satan. Have predetermined boundaries or limits when it comes to dealing with drugs. Those boundaries should be to go to all lengths to avoid them.

UNDERSTANDING THE BIGGER PICTURE.

Drugs are destroying Black communities and weakening the strength of the United States of America. The question has been asked: "Is there a conspiracy against Blacks and have drugs been used to do Blacks in?" Well it doesn't take a rocket scientist to figure out that drugs have always been sent to the ghetto. It was never intended for cocaine to hit the suburbs but if you dig one ditch, you had better dig two. The bigger picture shows that there are people who would like to destroy the Black community but they can only do it with our cooperation.

Planned Parenthood's goal in the beginning was to limit the number of undesirables (Blacks, and Hispanics) so they placed the abortion clinics in Black neighborhoods and made abortion free. The liquor companies don't place advertisements in the suburbs but in the Black communities so that the weak are constantly bombarded with visuals to stimulate their weaknesses. Morality in America in general, and in Black America particularly, is at an all time low.

So, the big picture is one of rapid moral, civil, social, and religious degeneration of a country which is affecting all. The greatest damage is being done to those who have the least power to resist, the minorities. The only redeeming fact in this whole scenario is that YOU CAN CHOOSE NOT TO PARTICIPATE IN THE DESTRUCTION.

I have decided that I am not going to be poor, illiterate, uneducated, deprived, abused, victimized, oppressive and many other things. In as much as I have control of my life and can do as I please, I have chosen the route of success and you can too.

A DRUG IS A DRUG IS A DRUG

Crack cocaine is not the only drug. Cigarettes, alcohol, snuff, and beer are all drugs. If you are addicted to one drug, you are no better than a person who is addicted to another drug. Don't seek to rate drugs according to their destructive qualities but according to their addictive qualities. I have been told that it is just as hard to get off of cigarettes as it is to get off of cocaine.

Remember that the only successful approach to drugs is to never introduce your body to them.

QUESTIONS
FOR INTROSPECTION AND DISCUSSION
(to make you think)

1. Are you committed to staying drug free? Yes____ No____

2. Do you see drugs as the enemy of you and your community? Yes____ No____

3. Are you developing coping mechanisms so that you will not need to find relief through drugs? Yes____ No____

   If so, name some of your coping mechanisms_____
   _____
   _____

4. How many people can you name who have been destroyed by drugs? _____

APPLICABLE SCRIPTURES

All things are lawful unto me, but all things are not expedient: all things are lawful for me, but I will not be brought under the power of any.

I Corinthians 6:12

Wine is a mocker, strong drink is raging: and whosoever is deceived thereby is not wise.

Proverbs 20:1

Hear thou, my son, and be wise, and guide thine heart in the way. Be not among winebibbers; among riotous eaters of flesh: For the drunkard and the glutton shall come to poverty: and drowsiness shall clothe a man with rags.

Proverbs 23:19-21

Pride goeth before destruction, and a haughty spirit before a fall.

Proverbs 16:18

He that is soon angry dealeth foolishly: and a man of wicked devices is hated.

Proverbs 14:17

Lest Satan should get an advantage of us: for we are not ignorant of his devices.

II Corinthians 2:11

Notes:_____

_____

_____

_____

_____

_____

_____

_____

_____

_____

_____

_____

_____

_____

PART THREE

YOU CAN PROSPER

CHAPTER NINE

My First Job

I HAD HUNG OUT IN THE MUSIC STORE FOR some time now. I loved music, played several instruments and loved to hang out in the store. On this particular day I was on my way to find a job when the store owner asked me what I was doing. I told him that I was on my way to get a job and he stated that I could work for him. This was a dream come true!

What I did not anticipate was Mr Pratt. Mr. Pratt was my immediate supervisor. Mr. Pratt was a White man about 6'2" tall and right at 300 pounds. At 15 years old, I was 120 pounds soaking wet. As I look back, I appreciate Mr. Pratt for he solidified many basic principles that my dad taught me which have contributed to my success in life.

I am going to share with you some basic things that young men need to incorporate into their success plans that I learned on my first job.

THE HAND SHAKE - (the fine line between firmness and arrogance)

In this world of fickleness there is a need for genuine commitments. When two men shake hands a lot of information is transmitted. A hand shake can tell you if a person is genuinely glad to meet you or if they are shaking just as a formality.

Mr. Pratt, my 6'2", 300lb. boss taught me how to shake hands when I was 15 years old. He met me as I came to work each day, extended his huge hand to me and shook it. His grip was almost unbearable. He would tell me: "When you shake a man's hand, look him in the eye!" I learned how to do that. After some practice I learned how to confidently

shake a man's hand who:
>•Was bigger than I was.
>•Held the power to fire me, and
>•Presented a challenge because of his high expectations of me.

The ability to shake hands properly can determine if you get a job, how others treat you, and it gives an indication of the spirit that lies within you. A famous blind musician stated that he could shake a woman's hand and tell how tall she was, how much she weighed, and the texture of her skin told him additional things. Well, I am not talking about shaking a woman's hand. I am talking about shaking a man's hand. Be careful to be genuine when you shake hands with someone because a discerning person can tell when you are not genuine. Also, don't overdo the macho hand shake. In other words don't try too hard to impress another man by squeezing his hand.

It is not how hard you squeeze his hand, it is simply being firm and genuine that conveys through your handshake a sense of purity of character that will impress men of integrity. Your hand shake can convey to some degree the content of your character.

THE IMPORTANCE OF BEING DEPENDABLE

Confidence in an unfaithful man in time of trouble is like a broken tooth, and a foot out of joint.
Proverbs 25:19

This proverb very accurately describes how it feels to be let down when you are depending on someone. An employer is dependant on those who work for him. Each man is like a link in a chain that depends on the strength of the other links to successfully complete the task at hand.

Just the other day I watched one of my favorite football teams in a play-off game. The score was tied with seconds to go and it was up to the punter to kick an easy field goal. He missed! His failure, though unintentional, let the whole team down. When someone depends on you, don't let them down. If you develop the discipline of being dependable you will have in your possession part of a strong foundation to build a successful life upon. Don't ever allow yourself to be like a <u>broken tooth or a foot out of joint.</u>

THE IMPORTANCE OF BEING PUNCTUAL

I resent the concept and term "CP time" which stands for "colored people's time." This idea promotes an old southern stereotype that Black people cannot be on time. Any event that I am involved in I strongly insist on starting on time. The reason is that it helps develop a positive attitude about what you are doing.

In the business world you don't get ahead by being on time, you get ahead by being **early**! Your punctuality speaks volumes about you before you ever open your mouth. When you are punctual people perceive you as:

1. Organized
2. Prepared
3. Anxious for the task at hand
4. A potential Leader

While in school be at least 3 minutes early for each class and take that time to get yourself together for the class. Please believe me when I tell you that teachers notice this and it will help you in the long run.

THE IMPORTANCE OF BEING TRUSTWORTHY

A wise servant shall have rule over a son that causeth shame, and shall have part of the inheritance among the brethren.
Proverbs 17:2

Not long ago a business in my town went bankrupt. The reason that the owner gave for going under was that his employees ripped him off. Employers are frantically searching for trustworthy employees to man their businesses. We live in an age when respect for the possessions of others is at an all time low. When you determine that you will be trustworthy you have increased your marketability. It is still possible to get a job and be promoted because you can be trusted. Trust is something that is invaluable.

A good name is rather to be chosen than great riches, and loving favour rather than silver and gold.
Proverbs 22:1

Here is a good place to make the point that it is important to establish yourself with a group of reputable, responsible persons who will attest to your trustworthiness. This can be done by establishing your integrity in school, becoming an active member in a local Church, some reputable civic organization or any affiliation that is positive. You never know when you will need people on your side.

Your first job is very important because it is the beginning of a lifetime of work. If you take the time to work on these basics that we are discussing, your working career will get off to a good start.

THE IMPORTANCE OF BEING PROFESSIONAL ON THE JOB

I stopped by a fast food restaurant the other day because I needed some food in a hurry. The brother who was flippin' the burgers was involved in a heated discussion with his woman about a problem they had the night before. I was not interested in their personal problems because I wanted a double burger, fries and a large drink (in a hurry). The brother stood there talking to his woman for at least 3 minutes (which is a long time) during the peak lunch time rush hour. Now, check this out: If I had been his boss, I would have fired the brother on the spot!! He was acting unprofessionally on the job. He was causing the customers to become dissatisfied which translates into lost funds for the business.

There is a time to talk to your woman, and it is not while you are being paid to work. I know that there are emergencies, but I am not talking about an emergency. What I am talking about is displaying the attitude that the boss should pay you regardless of how hard you work and how bad your attitude is. The bottom line is to give the man a good day's work for your pay. This is how you get ahead in life.

THE ABILITY TO BE ABLE TO TAKE A REBUKE

It amazes me how so many young people have so much pride that they cannot receive a rebuke (correction). A rebuke properly given is in your best interest. Let me say that I appreciate rebukes because I know that they are designed to eliminate future mistakes and pain.

Reprove not a scorner, lest he hate thee: rebuke a wise man, and he will love thee.

Proverbs 9:8

A wise son heareth his father's instruction: but a scorner heareth not rebuke.

Proverbs 13:1

Poverty and shame shall be to him that refuseth instruction: but he that regardeth reproof shall be honoured.

Proverbs 13:18

When a young person says: "Kaint no body tell me what to do but my momma!", that young person IS A FOOL! When the momma says: "Kaint nobody tell my baby what to do!", that momma is a fool. The wise person knows that rebukes come from all people. As an adult, I am frequently rebuked by children. Not long ago, I was worried about a situation. I was not trying to solve it, I was just worrying about it. A child said to me: "don't worry about it, it will be alright." I received the rebuke.

Rebukes come from a variety of sources, even strangers. Those who you come in contact with on a daily basis are in your life to help mold you. When their comments or criticisms are right, learn to listen to them and respond appropriately and you will be a wiser man in the end.

QUESTIONS
FOR INTROSPECTION AND DISCUSSION
(to make you think)

1. Have you had your first job yet?_____

2. On my first job, Mr. Pratt was on my case. Who was on your case on your first job?_____

3. I stated how I learned from Mr. Pratt, what did you learn from your situation?_____
_____

4. How do you shake hands with a male your own age?_____

5. How do you shake hands with a man who is more powerful than you are?_____

6. Tell the truth, shame the devil! Are you dependable?____

7. Can you be counted on to fulfill responsibilities that are not your favorite things to do? _____

8. What do you feel are some of the benefits of being on time? _____

9. Tell the truth, shame the devil! If you worked in a store and you were left all alone in the store with $200.00 cash, (that nobody knew about) could you be trusted?
   Yes_____ No_____
Please remember that it is normal to consider taking the money. That is called temptation, but because you know that

it is wrong, you don't take the money. That's called integrity and self control.

> *There hath no temptation taken you but such as is common to man: but God is faithful, who will not suffer you to be tempted above that ye are able; but will with the temptation also make a way to escape, that ye may be able to bear it.*
>
> *I Corinthians 10:13*

10. If you were picked up tonight by the police because you looked like the 5'9" Black male who robbed a little old lady today, how many people (with integrity, not your homeys) could come to the police station and say: "I KNOW HE DIDN'T DO IT!! Not this brother, you MUST!! have the wrong man!"

List the people:

A._____

B._____

C. _____
　　　　(use an additional sheet if you need to)

11. Are you able to take a rebuke when it is properly given? ___Yes ___ No

12. Can you think of a time when you refused a rebuke which you should have received?_____

APPLICABLE SCRIPTURES

Confidence in an unfaithful man in time of trouble is like a broken tooth, and a foot out of joint.

Proverbs 25:19

A wise servant shall have rule over a son that causeth shame, and shall have part of the inheritance among the brethern.

Proverbs 17:2

A good name is rather to be chosen than great riches, and loving favour rather than silver and gold.

Proverbs 22:1

Reprove not a scorner, lest he hate thee: rebuke a wise man, and he will love thee.

Proverbs 9:8

A wise son heareth his father's instruction: but a scorner heareth not rebuke.

Proverbs 13:1

Poverty and shame shall be to him that refuseth instruction: but he that regardeth reproof shall be honoured.

Proverbs 13:18

A fool despiseth his father's instruction: but he that regardeth reproof is prudent.

Proverbs 15:5

Notes:_____

_____

_____

_____

_____

_____

_____

_____

_____

_____

_____

_____

_____

_____

_____

_____

CHAPTER TEN

Your Concept Of The Work Ethic

A MAN OR YOUNG MAN WHO DOES NOT have a healthy work ethic is ruined, messed up, and going nowhere fast. A work ethic can be defined as "the knowledge and acceptance of the fact that work is necessary for survival." This ethic is in grave danger today.

One of the factors that has contributed to the demise of the work ethic is welfare and invisible dads. When a child grows up in a home in which a check comes in the mail each month and it comes without any effort on the part of his mother, this child will not see the immediate benefits of labor.

The concept of getting something for nothing can be more powerful than the concept of working for your money. In reality, what we see and experience generally has more influence than what we are told to do. So, in this sense welfare is bad because it has erased the work ethic from much of the younger generation of American youth.

I firmly believe that young people should be taught that if you are not willing to work for what you want then you won't get it. Let's look at some specific guidelines that will help you develop a good work ethic:

1. NOBODY OWES YOU ANYTHING!

For even when we were with you, this we commanded you, that if any would not work, neither should he eat.
I Thessalonians 3:10

Even your parents aren't required by God or the government to supply all of your wants, but only your needs (food, clothing, shelter, etc.). If you have had the benefit of a generous up bringing please note that it won't last. After I found out about Santa, my Christmas list almost disappeared. There is going to come a time in your life when nobody will foot your bill and you will have to decide to work or to steal.

My suggestion is that you develop a strong work ethic now so that you can survive in the future. I was blessed to have a father who was a jack-of-all trades. As a result I learned to paint, wax floors, cut grass, do basic carpentry and so forth. Let me make a RADICAL suggestion to you. Find an adult male and help him work.

Help him for FREE if you have to so that you can get some experience!

You will be the richer as a result. As an adult, I purchased a run-down house to remodel. I did the plumbing as a result of watching a plumber and the painting as a result of watching a painter.

I repeat, (in case you fainted the first time) find an adult to learn a skill from. Let me put it like this. Have you ever seen those pictures that people take with books in the background? The books are designed to make it look like a law library. Well, your brain is like a library with no books in it. Every time you learn something new, you place a new book on the shelf in the skills section of your brain's library.

Please note that all books are not the same, but everything that you learn in life represents a book in your mental library. Try to avoid placing worthless books on the shelves in your mind's library because in the future, all that you can get out of life will be based on what you have on the shelf in that library. I would like to repeat my radical statement: FIND AN ADULT MALE TO LEARN A SKILL FROM EVEN IF YOU HAVE TO WORK FOR FREE!!

2. EVALUATE WHAT YOU HAVE SEEN MODELED

When it comes to your work ethic you need to analyze what you have seen modeled while you were young. I can remember my dad coming home at the end of the day after a hard day of physical labor. On one particular day, my mother met him at the door and with a sad face informed him that we had no dinner. My dad sighed, looked at me and said: "Come on Bud, let's go." We then walked to one of his many side jobs; cleaned and cut grass for enough cash for dinner.

This memory is indelibly, irrevocably, ineffaceably, ineradicably stamped on my memory. In other words, I won't forget it. I was impressed with my dad and consider his example of true manhood one of my greatest assets. What about you? What did you see as a child?:

...Did your parents work?
...Did a check come to the house each month?
...Do you get angry when you think about the fact that you must work now in school and someday in the market place? As you ask yourself these questions you can begin to identify any unhealthy attitudes in your mind and then challenge them.

3. WORK HARD IN COLLEGE NOW OR WORK HARD FOR THE REST OF YOUR LIFE.

Our society values a college education. Though it is true that a college education does not guarantee a good job, it does give you a better chance of getting a good job than you have with just a high school diploma. With this in mind, it pays to suffer through college with the hopes of a better paying job after college. I guess this thought could be summarized by saying that you should work with a future goal in mind as opposed to working just for a check today. If you work just for a check today you limit your chances for advancement and may still be on the same level years from now.

4. NEVER QUIT A JOB FOR THESE REASONS
A. You don't like it.

This is not a good enough reason to quit a job. As a matter of fact, most of the jobs you will have in this life you won't like. So, it comes down to discipline. If you have a job, you should do a good job and exhibit a good attitude even if you don't like the job. When you do this, you develop skills which prepare you for a better job.

B. Somebody made you mad.

This is no reason to quit because no matter where you work, somebody will eventually make you mad. In some cases they will make you mad hoping that you will quit. God wants to use the situation even if it is UNFAIR to teach you, so don't quit!

C. You think they are prejudice.

Despite all the laws and attempts by our Government and the Church, prejudice is here to stay. Want to hear something that will surprise you? Even Black people are prejudice of other Black people so it is impossible to escape. The reality of the matter is that the work environment is usually a hostile environment where people are out for themselves. As a result of this, you will have problems whether they are racially motivated or not. Now that I am grown, I know of many situations where because of my youth I have accused a White man of being prejudice when I now realize that he was just doing his job. Be careful not to use a claim of prejudice as a crutch for your ineffectiveness.

D. You are the only Black.

In this situation you must learn to capitalize on this and not let it work against you. When I am in these situations I see myself as a teacher because everyone there will be taught by me. Staying in this environment will cause you to be alert and work for perfection, don't quit.!

5. NEVER QUIT UNTIL YOU HAVE ANOTHER JOB!

A. Always give proper notice before quitting.

This is very simply having a professional attitude about yourself. Not only is it a professional attitude but it is a polite attitude. Be considerate.

B. Don't burn bridges.

Young people too often leave a situation in anger, cussin' someone out, or doing something that would leave a bad memory in the minds of those at the job. This can work against you when you go to your next job. Employers talk and share the good and bad about past employees. Not only this, but you may need to go back to that previous employer in the future for employment or for a recommendation for another job.

God will honor you if you work hard on your job. Please realize that men may diss you for flippin' burgers but if you do it with the right attitude, you will get opportunities for advancement.

For promotion cometh neither form the east, nor from the west, nor from the south. But God is the judge: he putteth down one, and setteth up another.
Psalm 75:6,7

QUESTIONS
FOR INTROSPECTION AND DISCUSSION
(to make you think)

1. How would you describe your work ethic?_____

_____

2. Are you satisfied with your work ethic? ___ Yes ___ No

3. What have you been told by your mother about your work ethic?_____

4. What have you been told by teachers and others about your work ethic?_____

5. Tell the truth, shame the devil: Are you l-a-z-y?
   ___ Yes ___ No

6. If so, what do you plan to do about it?_____

7. Would you rather someone give you something or work for it?_____

8. Name five men that you know who display a good work ethic:

   _____

   _____

   _____

   _____

   _____

APPLICABLE SCRIPTURES

Go to the ant, thou sluggard; consider her ways, and be wise: Which having no guide, overseer, or ruler, Provideth her meat in the summer, and gathereth her food in the harvest. How long wilt thou sleep, O sluggard? when wilt thou arise out of thy sleep? Yet a little sleep, a little slumber, a little folding of the hands to sleep: So shall thy poverty come as one that travelleth, and thy want as an armed man.

Proverbs 6:6-11

He becometh poor that dealeth with a slack hand: but the hand of the diligent maketh rich. He that gathereth in summer is a wise son: but he that sleepeth in harvest is a son that causeth shame.

Proverbs 10:4,5

He that tilleth his land shall be satisfied with bread: but he that followeth vain persons is void of understanding.

Proverbs 12:11

The labour of the righteous tendeth to life: the fruit of the wicked to sin.

Proverbs 10:16

For even when we were with you, this we commanded you, that if any would not work, neither should he eat.

II Thessalonians 3:10

Notes:_____

_____

_____

_____

_____

_____

_____

_____

_____

_____

_____

_____

_____

_____

_____

CHAPTER ELEVEN

I Was Treated Unfairly Today (Prejudice)

RECENTLY, I WAS IN A MALL WITH MY TWO youngest children. On this particular day I had on a suit and tie and was dressed very professionally. As I approached the cosmetics' counter, I noticed a woman that I had previously worked with at the counter making a purchase.

This woman was a tall, attractive, White woman with blue eyes and flowing blond hair. I had worked with the woman every day for a number of years and I was more impressed with her character than I was with her carriage (body). As I approached her to say hello, her back was turned so I cleared my throat to get her attention. Upon seeing this, the sales lady dissed me. She frowned, looked at me and said: "Sir, go on down the aisle, just! go! on! down! the! aisle!" I was shocked.

My female associate standing at the counter not knowing what was going on turned around, saw me, smiled and we talked like two friends who had not seen each other for a while.

The question on the floor now is: What should I say to the sales lady who dissed me? With the look on her face you could have bought her with a wet food stamp. What should I say? WHAT SHOULD I SAY! Should I just walk away and forget that she said anything? Should I make a face? Should I walk away with my nose in the air? Or, should I diss her like she dissed me?

When you are treated unfairly you should seek to respond knowledgeably. A wise response is the best response because it will bring the most good from the situation.

In order to respond wisely there are some things you should consider first. To check yourself, ask yourself these questions before you respond:

> •Am I in a bad mood or having a bad day?
> •Did I do something wrong to provoke this person?

Regarding the other person, ask yourself these questions:
> •Is this person crazy?
> •Has this person been exposed to intelligent Black folks?
> •What would I have done if the situation was reversed?
> •How can I do the right thing and come out ahead in this situation?
> A proper assessment of the situation is necessary before you say anything.

> *He that keepeth his mouth keepeth his life: but he that openeth wide his lips shall have destruction.*
> *Proverbs 13:3*

The most effective way for you to help people realize that they have wronged you, is for you to let God show them. In my situation, the sales lady knew she was wrong. At that point, for me to say anything would have been anti-climatic. Nothing I could have said would have made her feel any worse than she felt nor further impress upon her how wrong she was. So, I suggest that the best approach is to let God fix it and don't plead your own case. This is not always easy, but I challenge you to look at history and see how people who were dissed eventually shined because the truth will eventually come forth.

If thou hast done foolishly in lifting up thyself, or if thou hast thought evil, lay thine hand upon thy mouth.
Proverbs 30:32

If thine enemy be hungry, give him bread to eat; and if he be thirsty, give him water to drink: For thou shalt heap coals of fire upon his head, and the LORD shall reward thee.
Proverbs 25:21-22

I know that kindness to people who are dissin' you may be a difficult concept to embrace but it clearly is the best policy. Well, what about those situations where the person is going off and it seems like there is no justice and the person seems to be getting away with it. Shouldn't I go off then?

If it be possible, as much as lieth in you, live peaceably with all men.
Romans 12:18

Let me confess for a minute. I don't want you to think that I don't struggle with what I am trying to share with you. Just the other day, I blew it. My day was not going well and I encountered a situation at the bank where it seemed like the teller was trying to diss me. Yes, I am sorry to say that I went off (a little bit) and said to the woman: "Is there a problem, I've been banking here for five years, IS THERE A PROBLEM!" As I write this I am still sorry that I went off (a little bit) on the teller. The bad thing is that my going off did not help me get my money any faster and now the people at the bank look at me funny.

I believe that the best way to handle ignorant people and abusive situations is to walk away from them. You should have enough self esteem and confidence to know that the actions of another person will not hurt you. The danger in saying something and not walking away is that the situation may escalate.

> *Surely the churning of milk bringeth forth butter, and the wringing of the nose bringeth forth blood: so the forcing of wrath bringeth forth strife.*
> *Proverbs 30:33*

When you provoke an ignorant (ignent), evil person, you are asking for more trouble. With men this can only lead to violence, bloodshed and death. Now, don't get me wrong. There is a time to fight and a time to die for what you know to be right but that time is not when someone hurts your feelings. If someone threatens your life or the life of your family, then is the time to protect yourself.

ANYTHING SHORT OF A LIFE THREATENING SITUATION SHOULD BE WALKED AWAY FROM!!

Remember, we live in a sin-sick, sin-cursed society. People will always diss other people. The question on the floor still remains: "How will you handle it?"

QUESTIONS
FOR INTROSPECTION AND DISCUSSION
(to make you think)

1. What did you do the last time you were treated unfairly?
   (explain)_____

   _____

2. When you are treated unfairly in school do you assess the situation before you go off? ___Yes___No

3. Have you dissed anybody lately? ___Yes___No

4. Are you secure enough in yourself to get dissed and ignore it? ___Yes___No

5. Do you really believe that people will reap what they sow? ___Yes___No

APPLICABLE SCRIPTURES

He that keepeth his mouth keepeth his life: but he that openeth wide his lips shall have destruction.
Proverbs 13:3

If thou hast done foolishly in lifting up thyself, or if thou hast thought evil, lay thine hand upon thy mouth.
Proverbs 30:32

If thine enemy be hungry, give him bread to eat; and if he be thirsty, give him water to drink: For thou shalt heap coals of fire upon his head, and the LORD shall reward thee.

Proverbs 25:21-22

If it be possible, as much as lieth in you, live peaceably with all men.

Romans 12:18

Surely the churning of milk bringeth forth butter, and the wringing of the nose bringeth forth blood: so the forcing of wrath bringeth forth strife.

Proverbs 30:33

CHAPTER TWELVE

A Proper Attitude About Money

A VERY POPULAR BIBLE VERSE IS OFTEN misquoted like this: "Money is the root of all evil." The verse, I Timothy 6:10a says: *"For the love of money is the root of all evil."* So, it is not money but the love of money that gets people into trouble. Please be advised that there is nothing inherently wrong with money. Money is AMORAL which means that it is not good and it is not bad. Money becomes a factor only if we have an unhealthy attitude about it.

When a man loves money, he becomes a candidate for all types of traps. A man's attitude about finances or money is a CRITICAL factor in his future success. Those who are crazy about getting money will take one of several courses:

1. BECOME A CROOK TO GET IT.

I am amazed at the many times I have had the opportunity to get money dishonestly. I have had opportunities to do almost everything wrong that you could think of. Most of you who read these pages will be presented with many opportunities to do wrong. What saves you at this point is what could be called internal restraints. Something inside of you that keeps you in check when you are tempted. One restraint that has always helped me when it comes to getting money illegally is the fact that I know if I get it illegally, I won't be able to keep it without a lot of sorrow. You may not see the sorrow immediately but it will come.

The blessing of the Lord, it maketh rich, and he addeth no sorrow with it.

Proverbs 10:22

Wealth gotten by vanity shall be diminished: but he that gathereth by labor shall increase.

Proverbs 13:11

Better is a little with righteousness than great revenues without right.

Proverbs 16:8

Those who get their money illegally will eventually suffer the consequences for their deeds.

2. WORK SO HARD THAT THEY FORGET GOD IN THE PROCESS.

Dig this. God will not let a Christian forget that HE is God. God will get your attention when you ignore Him while making your fortune. I have learned from experience that God loves you and wants to use you. He will not allow you to have money or possessions that take the focus off of Him. He has a way of allowing your money to evaporate like a drop of water on a hot summer sidewalk. Look at what this scripture says:

Ye have sown much, and bring in little; ye eat, but ye have not enough; ye drink, but ye are not filled with drink; ye clothe you, but there is none warm; and he that earneth wages earneth wages to put it into a bag with holes.

Haggai 1:6

What this scripture means is that the people were spending all of their money on their houses and were neglecting God's house, the church. When God is neglected He can bring a leanness to the situation. God can put holes in our money bags. So, workaholicism at the expense of a relationship with God will not solve your money problems.

3. THEY ALLOW THEIR QUEST FOR MONEY TO SEPARATE THEM FROM FAMILY AND FRIENDS.

He that is greedy of gain troubleth his own house; but he that hateth gifts shall live.

Proverbs 15:27

This is a common story of the man that works hard to give things to his family and neglects to give himself to his family. Children resent this later in life and the financial stability that is gained is not worth the loss of wife or children. Again, it is not the money that is bad but the love for that money that is destructive. So, the wise man disciplines himself regarding money.

Now, let's look at some common problem areas that young men have with money. The first area that I want to talk about is credit.

I remember when I was first granted credit privileges. I had never had much and now the man says: "All you have to do is sign on the dotted line and it is yours." Name it, sign on the dotted line and claim it. I got in big trouble fast. I had to pay for everything that I signed for. Look at what the Bible says about credit:

The rich ruleth over the poor, and the borrower is servant to the lender.

Proverbs 22:7

Any man, woman, boy or girl who does not know how to use credit will soon be a servant to Visa, Mastercharge or your favorite clothing store.

- Never sign for what you can pay for.
- Never buy it when you first see it. Always go back a day or two later after you've cooled off.
- Remember, they will smile when you sign for it but take you to court and sue you when you are late with your payment.

He who borrows becomes the servant. Seek to be a free man. I know there are times when we all borrow to buy big ticket items such as cars, homes, or college but it should never be for stuff we really don't need. Borrowing has been presented by credit card companies and others who loan money as glamorous but in reality it is not glamorous but a form of enslavement that we should seek to avoid.

LOANING TO FRIENDS

This is something that we should do if we can and if we feel that God wants us to. Consider these things before you loan to friends:

- Is it a legit' loan? Don't be afraid to ask a lot of questions.
- Be sure to pray about it. People can be good liars when it comes to getting money.
- Get a CLEAR understanding up front if this is a loan or a gift. People get amnesia from time to time.
- We should not charge Christians interest. If you take the money out of savings to loan it to them, you may ask them for what you lost in interest while it was out of the bank but no more than what you would have gotten from the bank. In other words, don't try to make money off of fellow Christians or friends who are in need.

BORROWING FROM FRIENDS

Friends who are always borrowing money will stretch the friendship to its limits. One who is constantly borrowing money gets on your nerves. If you borrow all of the time it gives others the indication that:

- You are a poor manager of money.
- You need to work harder.
- You need to get a better job.

Keep your friendships strong by sparing your friends the burden of supporting you financially.

CO-SIGNING

It is very risky to co-sign for others. This should be done with extreme caution. Ten years ago, I co-signed for a friend against the advice of my wife to the tune of $2,500.00 (two thousand five hundred dollars.) My friend paid two payments and I had to pay the rest while listening to my wife say: "I told you so." Tell people that you don't co-sign for others. Say it is a policy of mine. Many people will not understand this but you can't worry about that.

A man void of understanding striketh hands, and becometh surety in the presence of his friend.
Proverbs 17:18

This verse is saying that a man who does not know any better will become surety or co-sign for his friend.

COMPOUNDED INTEREST

I can vividly remember my childhood. We never seemed to have enough money. My dad often borrowed money from a local finance company. It seemed like he was always late with the payments. They were always calling and he never seemed to get them paid off. As an adult, I now understand what was going on. They were charging him a high interest rate that compounded. They used to call it <u>add on interest</u>. For example, he would borrow $300.00 to be paid back in one year. The interest was 21% annually which meant that on the day that he took out the loan he owed $363.00 total. So, when he paid his first payment of $30.25 which went to pay the interest, he had a balance of $332.75. At this rate it took forever to pay off the loan.

Let me give you another example of how interest works. A friend of mine purchased a new car with a sticker price of $16,500.00. When the sticker price is computed at 11% interest, the total cost of the car comes to $18,315.00. The first payment is $600.00; of which $432.00 is paid on the car and $168.00 is payment on the interest. So, the $168.00 goes to the Bank as interest and payment for services.

Now, please note this point: most Black people are on the wrong side of compounded interest! Look at this example of how you can use compound interest to your advantage. Let's say you are 15 years old and you save $5.00 a month or $60 per year at 6 % interest. Look at what your returns will be five, ten, fifteen, and twenty years from now. Look at the following figures and see how a compounded interest rate of 6% will work for you.

Amount Returned in:

Amount Saved	5 years	10 years	15 years	20 years
$5 a month or $60 a year	$338	$791	$1397	$2208

I want to encourage you to strive to make compounded

interest work for you by starting and developing consistent saving patterns NOW!

TITHING

To tithe means to give God 1/10 of your gross income. In the Christian church there are those who tithe and others who have a problem with this principle. I am not going to go into a long Theological discussion of the matter other than to say that I tithe and I have prospered financially. Please note that I am not rich but I have everything that I need and most of my wants. God does not need our money but what He does desire our obedience in the area of finances. When we tithe, He has our obedience and He is then free to bless us.

> *Will a man rob God? Yet ye have robbed me. But ye say, Wherein have we robbed thee? In tithes and offerings. Ye are cursed with a curse: for ye have robbed me, even this whole nation. Bring ye all the tithes into the storehouse, that there may be meat in mine house, and prove me now herewith, saith the Lord of hosts, if I will not open you the windows of heaven, and pour you out a blessing, that there shall not be room enough to receive it.*
> *Malachi 3:8-10*

WOMEN AND MONEY

Don't fall into the trap of thinking that you have to have a lot of money to get a good woman. A good woman is more impressed with your character than with your cash. A good woman values a man who has integrity more than the brother who can buy her everything. Please note that you should work hard to provide for yourself and a woman but never seek for cash to be the criteria by which a woman chooses you or you choose a woman.

QUESTIONS
FOR INTROSPECTION AND DISCUSSION
(to make you think)

1. Tell the truth, shame the devil! Do you love money?
Yes___No

2. Have you ever cheated someone out of money?
___Yes ___No

3. Do you consider God when you think about money?
___Yes___No

4. How many people owe you money right now? _____
What is your attitude toward them?_____
_____

5. What is the largest sum of money you have ever had in
your pocket at one time? $_____ Where is the
money now?_____

6. Who do you owe money to right now? _____
Do you plan to pay it back? Yes___ No___ Find a Bible
and look up Psalm 37:21

7. Do you give money freely to God? ____Yes___No. To the
poor? ___Yes____no.

8. Do you know an adult who will co-sign for your car?
___Yes___No.   Have you ever asked them to? _____
Would you understand if they said NO? _____

9. Can you imagine saving money even when you don't have enough? ___Yes ___No

10. What one concept in this chapter do you have the greatest problem with? _____
    What do you plan to do about it? Check one:
    ___A. Not adapt the concept as your own.
    ___B. Pray about it.
    ___C. Discuss it with an older wiser man?

APPLICABLE SCRIPTURES

The blessing of the Lord, it maketh rich, and he addeth no sorrow with it.
                                    Proverbs 10:22

Wealth gotten by vanity shall be diminished: but he that gathereth by labor shall increase.
                                    Proverbs 13:11

Better is a little with righteousness than great revenues without right.
                                    Proverbs 16:8

Ye have sown much, and bring in little; ye eat, but ye have not enough; ye drink, but ye are not filled with drink; ye clothe you, but there is none warm; and he that earneth wages earneth wages to put it into a bag with holes.
                                    Haggai 1:6

He that is greedy of gain troubleth his own house; but he that hateth gifts shall live.
                                    Proverbs 15:27

111

The rich ruleth over the poor, and the borrower is servant to the lender.

Proverbs 22:7

A man void of understanding striketh hands, and becometh surety in the presence of his friend.
Proverbs 17:18

Will a man rob God? Yet ye have robbed me. But ye say, Wherein have we robbed thee? In tithes and offerings. Ye are cursed with a curse: for ye have robbed me, even this whole nation. Bring ye all the tithes into the storehouse, that there may be meat in mine house, and prove me now herewith, saith the Lord of hosts, if I will not open you the windows of heaven, and pour you out a blessing, that there shall not be room enough to receive it.
Malachi 3:8-10

Notes:_____

_____

_____

_____

_____

_____

_____

CHAPTER THIRTEEN

The Kings's English And Employment

IWAS ASSISTING A YOUNG BROTHER WHO WAS in search of a job. He had put in applications all over town when one day he received a call at the Church because he didn't have a phone. I went and found him and took him to the prospective employer and stood there while the prospective employer talked to him. The employer asked him: "Why do you want to work here?" The brother replied: "I need a job." The employer continued to ask the brother questions and each answer was about the brother's personal problems and not about solving the problems of the potential employer. Needless to say, he didn't get the job.

The brother talked with his prospective employer as if he was talking with his homey in the hood. When a Black man does this, his value and worth in the eyes of his employer diminishes. Young people must learn that people are put at ease when you talk in a manner that they are comfortable with. I had the opportunity go to another country where the people talked differently than I do. It was very difficult to order food and to be understood and understand others. I was very glad to get back to the states where I could understand and be understood. Don't put your employer in a foreign country every time he tries to talk with you.

The ability to speak "Standard English" is a skill that will take you far in life and many young Black men don't see the value in it. Here are some things to consider:

1. STANDARD ENGLISH WILL GET YOU NOTICED AND LISTENED TO.

Not too long ago, I was at a local housing complex on a Saturday afternoon and I came up on a young man leaning against a car with a wine bottle in one hand and his woman in the other. As it so happened, I was waiting on someone and while waiting, I got into a conversation with the young man who was extremely cool, laid back, and in his own world. During the conversation, the brother looked at me and said something like this:

"Yo man, it be rough on the street
trying to get enough to eat
kids gettin' me down
don't wanna mess around
job's hard to find
got my woman on my mind
can't seem to get straight
got to stop and meditate
I'm going to give you the spiel
I know the real deal".........

He continued on and on and finally stopped. After he stopped, he hugged his woman, sat back and grinned taking pride in his linguistic accomplishment. I looked at him and said something like this:

"I understand that the vicissitudes of life can be contentious and contrary, assailing and assaulting the ego and retiring a man's monumental efforts to a condition of ignominious invalidation. I also understand that the daily doldrums of sustaining this diminutive existence can be very exasperating, but I conclude that to retreat into a cocoon of inebriation in an attempt to incapacitate and invalidate life's incessant blows will not be efficacious."

At this point the brother stood up straight, his

countenance (face) changed and he looked at me and said: "Who are you?" I told him who I was and he began to listen to the wisdom of one who was older and wiser than he was.

Now, I want you to realize that because of how I answered him, he wanted to know who I was. With my vocabulary, (which is accepted wherever the English language is spoken), I challenged the brother to perform on the world's stage rather than only on the stage in his head.

2. AN INCREASED VOCABULARY WILL POINT OUT TO YOU THAT THE WORLD IS A HUGE PLACE.

Many of the words we use come from other countries and maintain their native pronunciation. The word "kindergarten" is a German word that means the children's garden, however, in America, we never translated it for usage. There are other words which are transliterated, which means the spellings may differ somewhat but the pronunciation and meaning is nearly the same. The word Hallejuah (Praise the Lord) is one such word.

3. AN ENHANCED VOCABULARY WILL MAKE YOU WISE BEYOND YOUR YEARS.

Words stimulate thought and when you study their origins it gives you extra power when you use them. Every new word you learn opens the door to many other words and the cycle is endless.

4. AN ENHANCED VOCABULARY COMES FROM USING A DICTIONARY.

It is common knowledge that Malcolm X read the dictionary while in prison. It may be difficult to see the gain from such activity but stop and think of the great men who had significant vocabularies: Martin Luther King Jr., Jesse Jackson, and Thurgood Marshall, just to name a few, were men of significant vocabularies. These men could think on their feet because they had words to express their thoughts. We have many great young thinkers today who will never be great because they can't express their thoughts. The newspaper is another place to pick up additional words. Read the paper and write down all the new words you come in contact with.

5. AN ENHANCED VOCABULARY WILL HELP YOU GET BETTER GRADES IN SCHOOL AND WILL HELP YOU GET PROMOTED ON YOUR JOB.

The ability to articulate your thoughts is power and money in the bank. Think about this. Musicians struggle to get what they hear in their heads recorded on their new CD. Fashion designers struggle to get what they see, in a new dress, manufactured and on the rack. Athletes struggle to make the play that is in their mind work on the field. You and I struggle to get what we are thinking out of our minds into our conversation. An enhanced vocabulary will help you get those valuable thoughts conveyed to other people. When this happens, you become more valuable, and wise in the sight of others.

6. EACH FIELD OF STUDY (DISCIPLINE) HAS IT'S OWN VOCABULARY.

Doctors talk doctor talk, lawyers talk lawyer talk, and so forth. I was impressed the last time I was in the court room by the vocabulary that was used there. I know a preacher who can take words and paint a picture so vividly that everyone in the congregation can see the picture. The other day I put my car in the shop. I told the mechanic that there was a low point on the front disc and that the disc needed to be turned. I LOVE to be able to speak the vocabulary of whatever we are talking about. Sometimes life forces us to learn new terms (vocabulary).

If you notice the handsome picture on the back of the book, you will see that this handsome author is bald. Well, my hair fell out after a very stressful period in my life. When this happened I had to learn a new term, "Alopecia." This term is what doctors use for baldness. My condition was alopecia totalis which means bald all over. My hair is now beginning to grow back so my condition has become *alopecia areata* which means bald in some areas.

When I buried my father, I talked to the funeral director who had a whole new vocabulary: embalming, vaults, sealers, visitation, expired, etc. I pray that you have a good vocabulary, other than what is common on the streets. You need a street vocabulary but you also need to be knowledgeable of the vocabulary of various disciplines or professions.

7. IN ADDITION TO ENHANCING YOUR VOCABULARY, LEARN THE PROPER STRUCTURE OF THE ENGLISH LANGUAGE.

If you are a citizen of the U.S.A., English is your official language. While there are numerous dialects, standard English is what's completely accepted. Discipline yourself and master the fundamentals of effective communication which include subject-verb agreement, proper use of adverbs, adjectives, and prepositional phrases.

QUESTIONS
FOR INTROSPECTION AND DISCUSSION
(to make you think)

1. When was the last time you learned a new word?_____What was that word?_____

2. Name someone of your age who has a impressive vocabulary._____

3. How many vocabularies or disciplines can you speak in?_____

4. Can you talk to a professional person without feeling intimidated? ___Yes___No

5. State your specific plans to increase your vocabulary.

_____

APPLICABLE SCRIPTURES

For my mouth shall speak truth; and wickedness is an, abomination to my lips.
Proverbs 8:7

A man's gift maketh room for him, and bringeth him before great men.
Proverbs 18:16

Let your speech be always with grace, seasoned with salt, that you may know how ye ought to answer every man.
Colossians 4:6

How forcible are right words: but what doth your arguing reprove?

Job 6:25

And Samuel grew, and the Lord was with him, and did let none of his words fall to the ground.

I Samuel 3:19

The words of the Lord are pure words: as silver tried in a furnace of earth, purified seven times.

Psalm 12:6

Notes:_____

_____

_____

_____

_____

_____

_____

_____

_____

Notes:_____

_____

_____

_____

_____

_____

_____

_____

_____

_____

_____

_____

_____

_____

_____

_____

PART FOUR

WHO'S IN CONTROL?

CHAPTER FOURTEEN

The Importance Of Controlling Your Passions And Not Letting Them Control You.

I WAS CALLED BY A FRIEND TO GIVE HIS ELDerly father a ride one day. After I picked his father up it soon became apparent to me that the old man wanted to talk. He proceeded to expound on issues of life that he felt needed to be addressed. At one point he said something that I distinctly remember. He said, "There are three things that will kill you: women, money, and alcohol."

I later thought about what he said and I feel that it is true but I also would like to state that it is an unbridled (uncontrolled) passion toward these things that is deadly.

Men have been destroyed for centuries because they could not control their passions. When I speak of passion the mind automatically drifts toward sex. Passion is much broader than that, but because our society focuses on sex we need to be aware of the danger of **undisciplined** sexual passion.

There is a danger in not controlling your sexual passion. Unbridled sexual passion affects you in these ways:

1. UNBRIDLED PASSION IMPAIRS DECISION MAKING.

When you are in love you don't think straight. When your passions are out of control, you don't think at all. Many men have made decisions in the heat of passion that controlled them for the rest of their lives. I was talking to a man the other day whose wife is making his life miserable.

He married her based on the passion that he had for her when he first met her.

2. UNBRIDLED PASSION IMPAIRS YOUR VISION.

When you are passionately looking at a woman, what you see is not what you see. What you see is being airbrush painted in your mind to make it look better. This is why they turn the lights down low in the night club. They want the red lights, yellow lights, blue lights, and black lights to alter what things look like so that what you see is not really what you see. Never make a decision about a woman while viewing her through the eyes of passion.

3. UNBRIDLED PASSION PROMOTES SITUATION ETHICS.

Situation Ethics is when right and wrong are based on the situation or what looks good now. Passion has its own way of thinking which usually goes like this: "Anything that feels this good can't be wrong." In the heat of passion, a man will say anything, promise anything, because the focus is on how to master the present situation.

4. UNBRIDLED PASSION IS IGNORANT OF CONSEQUENCES.

Unbridled passion clouds your ability to see and think about tomorrow. In the heat of passion caution is tossed to the wind.

5. UNBRIDLED PASSION SHOULD BE SAVED FOR YOUR WIFE.

Your unleashed passion should be saved for you wife. The Bible teaches that the marriage bed is the place where you can go at it.

Marriage is honourable in all, and the bed undefiled:
but whoremongers and adulterers God will judge.
Hebrews 13:4

HOW TO COOL YOUR PASSIONS

1. DON'T EXCITE THEM IN THE FIRST PLACE.

Don't involve yourself in sexually exciting activities. Pick the movies that you go to very carefully. Not only avoid X-Rated movies but avoid X-Rated music also. These things only excite your passions. Reading Playboy or a girlie magazine is equivalent to a child reading a comic book. Both are fantasy. There are many beautiful young women out there and looking at them is not a sin. The Bible says that Rebecca, Isaac's wife was pleasant to gaze upon. It is OK to look at women but don't undress them with your eyes. Jesus knew men very well because he said:

> *But I say unto you, That whosoever looketh on a*
> *woman to lust after her hath committed adultery with*
> *her already in his heart.*
> *Matthew 5:28*

Realize that passion comes from the inside so it must be controlled from there. It can be fueled from the outside but not controlled from the outside.

2. FORTIFY YOURSELF WITH THE OBJECTIVE TRUTH OF GOD.

One of the best defenses I know of is a strong offense. Your best offense is Scripture memorization. Let me tell you how you benefit from Scripture memorization. Take the following steps:

Step 1 Memorize some Scriptures.

Step 2 You are confronted with a perplexing problem, test or temptation.

Step 3 Your flesh wants to make a decision.

Step 4 The Holy Spirit searches the files in your mind to find the most appropriate Scripture.

Step 5 The Holy Spirit displays that Scripture on the computer screen in your mind.

Step 6 With both choices in clear view, you decide if you want to please yourself or please God and then you make the appropriate decision.

Let me see if I can make it clearer.

Step 1 You memorize Scripture to help you specifically with your passion.

Step 2 While minding your own business you start thinking about sex and the video with girlfriend, the Rap artist, doin' her thing and one thought leads to another. The next thing you know your passions are off to the races.

Step 3 Because you have memorized Scripture, the Holy Spirit comes in early during the temptation process, and searches the files of your mind. These Scriptures come to mind which will settle you down if you listen to them:

> *For the lips of a strange woman drop as an honeycomb, and her mouth is smoother than oil: But her end is bitter as wormwood, sharp as a twoedged sword. Her feet go down to death; her steps take hold on hell.*
>
> *Proverbs 5:3-5*

Hearken unto me now therefore, O ye children, and attend to the words of my mouth. Let not thine heart decline to her ways, go not astray in her paths. For she hath cast down many wounded: yea, many strong men have been slain by her. Her house is the way to hell, going down to the chambers of death.

Proverbs 7:24-27

Now concerning the things whereof ye wrote unto me: It is good for a man not to touch a woman. Nevertheless, to avoid fornication, let every man have his own wife, and let every woman have her own husband.

I Corinthians 7:1-2

3. DON'T STAY SINGLE FOREVER.

Listen to this: **The only sex that God smiles upon is when your are married.**

A. THE BIBLE SAYS THAT TO IS BETTER TO MARRY THAN TO BURN WITH PASSION. Please note that some people have the gift of singleness, God has made them to not need sex. If that is the way you are, don't worry about marriage. If you don't have the gift then you should plan to some day get married and have a wonderful sex life. If you have the gift, don't worry about getting married.

B. CHILDREN NEED A MOTHER AND FATHER IN THE HOME. You need to be a responsible man and accept the challenge to sacrificially love your wife and your children. Too many men are wimping out on their family. Don't take the easy way out. Ask God to help you grow into a nurturing responsible man.

C. NEVER MESS WITH ANOTHER MAN'S WIFE! NEVER! NEVER! NEVER! Go find Tyson, Holyfield, or Foreman and smack them in the face, but

DON'T mess WITH A MAN'S WIFE!!! When you get married, **DON'T FOOL AROUND!** It is impossible to fool around and not suffer DEARLY in the end. Oh, yeah!, It will be fun at first but in the end, in the end, in the end. The Bible acknowledges that it will be fun at first.

> *Stolen waters are sweet, and bread eaten in secret is pleasant.*
>
> *Proverbs 9:17*

> *Can a man take fire in his bosom, and his clothes not be burned? Can one go upon hot coals, and his feet not be burned? So he that goeth in to his neighbor's wife; whosoever toucheth her shall not be innocent. But whoso committeth adultery with a woman lacketh understanding: he that doeth it destroyeth his own soul. A wound and dishonor shall he get; and his reproach shall not be wiped away. Jealousy is the rage of a man: therefore he will not spare in the day of vengeance. He will not regard any ransom; neither will he rest content, though thou givest many gifts.*
>
> *Proverbs 6:27-29;32-35*

There is no escaping the consequences of having sex with another man's wife. The Bible very accurately declares that the husband will be enraged when he finds out about it. No present or gift will cool his anger.

I want to also warn you to avoid the aggressive married woman who wants to find some action with a young man. Unfortunately this is very common today.

For by means of a whorish woman a man is brought to a piece of bread: and the adultress will hunt for the precious life.

Proverbs 6:26

When it comes to avoiding the traps that women will set for you it is important to remember these things:

1. Don't listen to her rap. *Proverbs 6:24 says: "To keep thee from the evil woman, from the flattery of the tongue of a strange woman."* It is not wise to let a woman talk to you in a seductive manner. Most men don't handle that very well.

2. Don't think on her beauty in your mind. *Proverbs 6:25a says: "Lust not after her beauty in thine heart;"* You are vulnerable to what you think about. If you think on her beauty it may cause you to weaken in her presence. You will unknowingly give her more credibility than she deserves.

3. Don't stare her in the face. *Proverbs 6:25b "neither let her take thee with her eyelids."* A woman's eyes are powerful weapons against a young man. Some older men can look them in the eyes and let them cry, but most young men can't handle it.

QUESTIONS
FOR INTROSPECTION AND DISCUSSION
(to make you think)

1. On a scale of 1 to 10 with 10 being the greatest, how good are you at controlling your passions?_____

2. Have you ever started watching a movie and turned it off or left when you decided that it was inappropriate material?
   ___Yes___No

3. What do you do when you have problems with your passion? Do you let it fly or do you challenge it?
   ___fly___challenge

4. Do you fantasize about being with a beautiful woman?
   ___Yes___No

5. Do you realize the importance of working to control not only your thoughts of passion but all thoughts?
   ___Yes___No

6. Did you realize that TV and the movies saturate us with sex not because it is good for us but because IT SELLS!?
   ___Yes___No

7. List five results or consequences of not controlling your anger.
   1._____
   2._____
   3._____
   4._____
   5._____

8. Can you see through the lie that TV presents when it shows passion with no consequences? ___Yes___No

APPLICABLE SCRIPTURES

Keep thy heart with all diligence for out of it are the issues of life.

Proverbs 4:23

The heart is deceitful above all things, and desperately wicked: who can know it?

Jeremiah 17:9

He that hath no rule over his own spirit is like a city that is broken down, and without walls.

Proverbs 25:28

Let not sin therefore reign in your mortal body, that ye should obey it in the lusts thereof.

Romans 6:12

All things are lawful unto me, but all things are not expedient: all things are lawful for me, but I will not be brought under the power of any.

I Corinthians 6:1

For a whore is a deep ditch; and a strange woman is a narrow pit.

Proverbs 23:27

Notes:_____

_____

_____

_____

_____

_____

_____

_____

_____

_____

_____

_____

_____

_____

_____

CHAPTER FIFTEEN

How To Avoid The Lure Of Homosexuality

THE INCREASE IN THE TREND OF MEN having sex with men in the Black community is having a serious negative impact on the Black family. When a man decides to live this way, some of the results are:

> •One less man to lead a Black household
> •One more negative example for our youth.
> •One more potential AIDS victim.
> •One more life that will be severely scarred by sin.

I feel very strongly about this issue and speak unreservedly about it. The homosexual lifestyle is one that young men should avoid at all costs. It is one of many paths to a miserable life.

Well, let's look at how to avoid the lure of homosexuality. First of all we need to guard against the internal lure and the external lure. There are those who will tell you that they were "born gay." This statement disagrees with what secular studies have said and with what God has said:

> *So God created man in his own image, in the image of God created he him; male and female created he them.*
>
> *Genesis 1:27*

So, according to God, no man is born gay. But it is true that all men are born with certain **BENTS, WEAKNESSES, TENDENCIES OR AREAS OF SUSCEPTIBILITY** that could lead one to believe that he was born a certain way. For example there are people who seem to have been born to steal. Look at why we say this:

- They are good at it.
- They seem to do it with no guilty feelings.
- They show no desire to change and it seems like they will never change.

All these things being true, I still don't believe that they were born thieves. The brother who is a compulsive womanizer feels that he was made that way. He gets married and cheats on his wife and feels that it is something that he was made to do.

This brother has a **PREDISPOSITION, A PROCLIVITY, A PREFERENCE** toward that behavior and he is not about to change. What about the brother that has a tendency toward laziness? This brother feels that it is OK to sponge off of his woman. He feels that this is natural and he has no intention of changing. He has a **PREDISPOSITION, A PROCLIVITY, A PREFERENCE** toward that behavior.

These people were not made that way but they may have **PRIVATE PASSIONS, PREDISPOSITIONS, AND PREFERENCES** that make it difficult for them to kick certain habits. These bents can be considered internal lures. Please note:

JUST BECAUSE YOU MAY HAVE AN UNNATURAL ATTRACTION TO MEN DOES NOT MEAN THAT YOU WERE BORN GAY!

Just like any weakness in any area, you must decide that it is fundamentally wrong and not do it. I want you to know today that every successful adult Black male has had a weak area that he had to overcome or that he is still fighting to overcome. This weakness would destroy this man if he ever allowed himself to be overtaken by it. So, the internal lure of homosexuality needs to be dealt with. This internal lure could be the result of several things:

1. Sexual abuse at the hands of a man. If you have been abused by a man, you need to talk about it with your pastor or CHRISTIAN counsellor. To keep it inside only allows the thief to work undetected. Talking will turn the light on and expose the negative trends that may be developing subconsciously.

2. Unprocessed hurts from the past. When something bad happens to us we need to process it (cry, yell, hurt, hate, but finally heal). If this is not done, these subconscious hurts from the past will control you and result in weird behavior.

3. Early exposure to pornography. When little children are exposed to pornography it affects them adversely and may lead them to pursue perverted sex.

4. Satanic suggestion. Satan deals with us through suggestions. Have you ever had a thought go through your mind that you totally disagreed with, knew was wrong, didn't want to have anything to do with, yet you kept thinking it? That is satan yelling in your ear. His suggestions are easy to identify because they are wrong, usually perverted, involve intrigue, suspense, and the penalty is usually hidden from you. I find it very interesting that the Bible acknowledges that when a married man has an affair with another man's wife it can be **temporarily** fun. The Bible also clearly states that in the end there will be devastation.

> *Stolen waters are sweet, and bread eaten in secret is pleasant.*
> *Proverbs 9:17*

So, the thing to do is to test all of your bright ideas against the Word of God and you will be able to tell if it is a bright idea or a satanic suggestion.

The external lure of homosexuality has to do with the traps that are set in our society by circumstance and by design. A young man whose body has just matured to the point where he desires to have sex must be careful. The reason for this is that he has limited or no sexual experience to guide him during this period of heightened sexual pressure. During this period of life there are some things that a young man should never do:

1. Never masturbate in a crowd. Masturbation or self release is something that you want to avoid doing. If you decide to masturbate, never do it with other guys. There are many reasons for this.

- Someone may decide to assist you and at this point it becomes homosexuality.
- You should seek to avoid being nude around men when they are sexually aroused and they want to make you an object of their lust.
- The sex act is a period of intense emotional, physical, and spiritual excitement and should never be publicized.

2. Avoid company with groups of aggressive homosexual men. One thing that the TV doesn't show is the aggressive violent side of the "gay" world. In the right setting, homosexual men will forcefully restrain and sodomize (have abnormal sexual intercourse, e.g. anal intercourse) another man. Male on male rape is not at all uncommon. When I was in high school I had a friend who played football. He told me that one of the most muscular men on the team would look at a smaller player and tell him: "I'm going to #@*& you." And he meant it too! It is most interesting that because of his lifestyle, this individual was killed before he was 21 years old. Who knows how many men he damaged before his death?

Another problem in the Black community is the Black man returning from prison who has been victimized. It is very unfortunate when this happens because that man will never be the same and will need counselling and prayer to fully recover his manhood.

3. Guard against a subtle change in your mindset. Because of our society's acceptance of same sex intercourse, many people find it no longer offensive. In order to guard yourself, wrong must stay wrong and right must stay right. There is an old saying which goes like this: **"WRONG IS WRONG EVEN IF EVERYBODY DOES IT AND RIGHT IS RIGHT EVEN IF NOBODY DOES IT."** Homosexuality is one of many perils that young men must guard against. What makes it dangerous is that many seek to convince society that it is normal, natural, acceptable behavior.

One hundred years ago lying, stealing, homosexuality, murder, adultery, fornication, beastiality, were wrong and they are still wrong today. I will admit that in the United States of America you have the right to do all of these things but you will suffer now and God is sitting at the cross roads of time with additional consequences in the life to come. Many acts may be legal, but that does not make them moral. Today there are those who seek to remove homosexuality from the wrong list and proclaim that those old standards don't apply here. Listen to how the timeless truth of how the Bible describes homosexuality:

> ***ABOMINATION*** - *Thou shalt not lie with mankind, as with womankind: it is abomination.*
> *Leviticus 18:22*

> ***AGAINST NATURE*** - *For this cause God gave them up unto vile affections: for even their women did change the natural use into that which is against nature:*
> *Romans 1:27*

> ***UNSEEMLY*** - *And likewise also the men, leaving the natural use of the woman, burned in their lust one toward another; men with men working that which is unseemly, and receiving in themselves that recompense of their error which was meet.*
> *Romans 1:27*

The bottom line is that you should seek to avoid the lure of homosexuality. Anything that a man wants bad enough, he can justify. Anything that a man wants to avoid bad enough, God will help him avoid. Resolve to grow to **UNTAINTED MANHOOD** with God's help.

THE EFFEMINATE BLACK MALE

Let me mention something that applies here. A young

man should seek to deal with any glaring effeminate traits that he has picked up over the years. It is easy and natural for a young boy who has been raised by his mother to pick up many of her habits. Usually, most of the glaring feminine moves, looks, attitudes and words are dropped when the young man goes to school and socializes with the other boys. In other cases, the boy will hold on to these traits too long. When this happens, the effeminate youth attracts the attention of older homosexual men who will seek to induct and introduce the young man into a life of homosexuality.

HOMOSEXUALITY, AIDS, AND THE BLACK COMMUNITY

AIDS is spreading in the Black community at an alarming rate. One of the reasons for this is the closet Black homosexual. I have known many Black men who have struggled with the lure of homosexuality. Some of these men had wives and children. I know of some men who had fiiii-ne women yet they struggled with a desire for men.

As I look back and analyze those men who struggled with this I become aware that they tried to keep their women or families. Only a couple of these Black men went all out for men. Black men have a tendency to keep their homosexuality in the closet.

The result of this for the Black community and the Black woman in particular is that heterosexual AIDS infections in the Black community are extremely high.

The homosexual lifestyle is unhealthy for our nation and as young men and mature men we should stand and reject the "gay" influence in our personal lives, Churches, community and nation. History shows that nations which embraced the homosexual lifestyle were in their last stages of decline. I pray that you will resolve to agree with God on this issue and order your life accordingly.

QUESTIONS
FOR INTROSPECTION AND DISCUSSION
(to make you think)

1. Name 5 successful Black men who you know are Successfully dealing with their bents._____

_____

_____

2. What negative personal bent do you have that you are aware of that needs to be dealt with?_____

3. Do you display feminine characteristics?
   Yes_____No_____
   If so, what do you plan to do about them?_____

4. Do you know any homosexual young men?
   Yes_____ No_____
   If so, would you feel comfortable talking to them and trying to help them see how they are making a mistake?
   Yes_____No_____

APPLICABLE SCRIPTURES

But evil men and seducers shall wax worse and worse, deceiving, and being deceived.

II Timothy 3:13

Thou shalt not lie with mankind, as with womankind: it is abomination.

Leviticus 18:22

For this cause God gave them up unto vile affections: for even their women did change the natural use into that which is against nature:

Romans 1:27

And likewise also the men, leaving the natural use of the woman, burned in their lust one toward another; men with men working that which is unseemly, and receiving in themselves that recompense of their error which was meet.

Romans 1:27

Notes:_____

_____

_____

_____

_____

_____

_____

_____

_____

_____

CHAPTER SIXTEEN

The Woman, A Man's Greatest Test

S ON IF YOU REALLY WANT TO BE A MAN, learn how to treat a woman. Dealing with a woman "WISELY" is one of the greatest tasks that any man will face in his whole life! The reason this is the case is because a woman is different from a man. Women have bigger brains, sharper senses, and they live longer. Not only this, but a woman carries her feelings as a chip on her shoulder. She is emotionally more transparent than a man. Men today are attempting to treat women and relate to them as they do other men. This is very unwise.

LOVE EQUALS MOTIVATION

God made a woman to respond to love. The Bible tells the man to LOVE his wife. When a woman is loved she is at her best. For years men have discovered the woman's need for love and exploited that need. It is a terrible thing for a man to worm, work and wiggle his way into a woman's heart by telling her that he loves her and then using love or what she perceives as love to keep her while he is unfaithful. It is a terrible thing when a man uses love which is so dear and intimate to a woman for anything other than sincere purposes.

The fact that love is such a motivator for women is common knowledge to most men. The problem comes in the fact that we don't capitalize on it in a positive way. A man must learn to love a woman even when she is unlovely (evil).

When she is loved, she will be motivated to be all that she can be.

HER BODY EQUALS FLUCTUATION

Listen very carefully. You don't know anything about a woman's body until you have lived with one for a while. Even then you haven't seen anything until you go through nine months of pregnancy and view the delivery of a baby.

Each woman goes through four seasons in a month: spring, summer, fall and winter. These seasons are related to her monthly cycle and correspond to chemical fluctuations (hormones) in her system. The fluctuations vary from woman to woman but all women fluctuate to some degree. In most cases there is a direct correlation between this chemical fluctuation and her moods, energy level and sex drive. If a man does not understand these fluctuations and where his woman is at any given time, he may have a hard time relating to her wisely.

Back a few years ago men were more in touch with nature and were more knowledgeable of the woman's monthly cycle.

YOUR STRENGTH EQUALS STABILIZATION

A woman needs for a man to be consistent and stable. When a woman fluctuates she needs stability on the part of her man. In most relationships it takes the woman and the man a few years to understand this dynamic. Once this is understood it makes for a better relationship, one in which there is understanding and support.

> *Likewise, ye husbands, dwell with them according to knowledge, giving honor unto the wife, as unto the weaker vessel, and as being heirs together of the grace of life; that your prayers be not hindered.*

Never be satisfied with the amount of knowledge you have about your woman. Seek additional wisdom and knowledge from God, your woman, and an older man.

> *Wisdom is the principal thing; therefore get wisdom: and with all thy getting get understanding.*
>
> *Proverbs 4:7*

> *Give instruction to a wise man, and he will be yet wiser: teach a just man, and he will increase in learning.*
>
> *Proverbs 9:9*

THREE THINGS THAT ALL WISE YOUNG MEN SHOULD AVOID

1. MARRIED WOMEN

Any young man who messes with a married woman is very foolish. When you do this, God is against you, the husband is against you and society frowns on it.

> *Wherefore they are no more twain, but one flesh. What therefore God hath joined together, let not man put asunder.*
>
> *Matthew 19:6*

> *But whoso committeth adultery with a woman lacketh understanding: he that doeth it destroyeth his own soul. A wound and dishonor shall he get; and his reproach shall not be wiped away. For jealousy is the rage of a man: therefore he will not spare in the day of vengeance. He will not regard any ransom; neither will he rest content, though thou givest many gifts.*
>
> *Proverbs 6:32-35*

Unfortunately there are older married women who will entice young men with money, cars and sex. It is in your best interest to stay away from it all.

My son, if sinners entice thee, consent thou not.
Proverbs 1:10

2. AVOID THE FOOLISH WOMAN

Many men will hook up with a foolish woman because there is very little challenge there. Many foolish women are easy to get over on so brothers go that way because they don't have to work so hard.

A foolish woman is clamorous: she is simple, and knoweth nothing. For she sitteth at the door of her house, on a seat in the high places of the city, To call passengers who go right on their ways: Whoso is simple, let him turn in hither: and as for him that wanteth understanding, she saith to him, Stolen waters are sweet, and bread eaten in secret is pleasant. But he knoweth not that the dead are there; and that her guests are in the depths of hell.
Proverbs 9:13-18

The danger with foolish women is you can get stuck with any woman you date. **ANY WOMAN YOU DATE MAY BECOME YOUR MATE!** If you have sex with her, you become one flesh and she will be in your bloodstream for at least 5 years. The best approach is to avoid this woman altogether.

3. AVOID THE WICKED WOMAN

There is nothing more dangerous than a wicked woman. As our society becomes more wicked, the women of our society will become more wicked. This scripture applies to women and men:

> *But evil men and seducers shall wax worse and worse, deceiving, and being deceived.*
>
> *II Timothy 3:13*

A wicked woman will lay a trap for a young man. Generally the young man is partially blinded by the woman's beauty and is not able to make good decisions. A wicked woman will use her sexual powers to seduce the man and render him helpless. As old and wise as I am, I still avoid wicked women like the plague.

> *For the commandment is a lamp; and the law is light; and reproofs of instruction are the way of life: To keep thee from the evil woman, from the flatter of the tongue of a strange woman. Lust not after her beauty in thine heart; neither let her take thee with her eyelids. for by means of a whorish woman a man is brought to a piece of bread: and the adulteress will hunt for the precious life.*
>
> *Proverbs 6:23-26*

God has given men and women to each other to build up and complete each other. If wisdom is not used and Godly advise followed there can be great suffering.

> *Marriage is honorable in all, and the bed undefiled: but whoremongers and adulterers God will judge.*
>
> *Hebrews 13:4*

QUESTIONS
FOR INTROSPECTION OR DISCUSSION
(to make you think)

1. Do you have a girlfriend? ___Yes ___No

2. Does she fluctuate? ___Yes ___No

3. Are you consistent when she fluctuates? ___Yes ___No

4. Are you prepared to love a woman constantly?
   ___Yes ___No

5. Have you ever been tempted by a foolish woman?
   ___Yes ___No If yes, what did you do? _____

6. Have you ever been tempted by a wicked woman?
   ___Yes ___No If yes, what did you do? _____

7. Have you ever been tempted by a married woman?
   ___Yes ___No If yes, what did you do? _____

8. Do you know an older spiritual man who can help you understand women? ___Yes ___No

9. What one question would you like to have answered?

_____

_____

APPLICABLE SCRIPTURES

The mouth of strange women is a deep pit: he that is abhorred of the Lord shall fall therein.

Proverbs 22:14

Likewise, ye husbands, dwell with them according to knowledge, giving honor unto the wife, as unto the weaker vessel, and as being heirs together of the grace of life; that your prayers be not hindered.

I Peter 3:7

Wisdom is the principal thing; therefore get wisdom: and with all thy getting get understanding.

Proverbs 4:7

Give instruction to a wise man, and he will be yet wiser: teach a just man, and he will increase in learning.

Proverbs 9:9

Wherefore they are no more twain, but one flesh. What therefore God hath joined together, let not man put asunder.

Matthew 19:6

But whoso committeth adultery with a woman lacketh understanding: he that doeth it destroyeth his own soul. A wound and dishonor shall he get; and his reproach shall not be wiped away. For jealousy is the rage of a man: therefore he will not spare in the day of vengeance. He will not regard any ransom; neither will he rest content, though thou givest many gifts.

Proverbs 6:32-35

149

My son, if sinners entice thee, consent thou not.
Proverbs 1:10

For the commandment is a lamp; and the law is light;
and reproofs of instruction are the way of life: To
keep thee from the evil woman, from the flatter of the
tongue of a strange woman. Lust not after her beauty
in thine heart; neither let her take thee with her
eyelids. for by means of a whorish woman a man is
brought to a piece of bread: and the adulteress will
hunt for the precious life.
Proverbs 6:23-26

Notes:_____

_____

_____

_____

_____

_____

_____

_____

_____

CHAPTER SEVENTEEN

How To Overcome Controlling Sexual Thoughts About Women

WHEN I WAS IN JR. HIGH SCHOOL, I HAD A paper route. I never will forget the Tuesday evening that I was collecting from my customers and something happened that really shook me up.

As I passed a particular apartment building on the lower level, I saw something that caused my 8th grade mind go into a melt down. There was a young lady who was dressing and she could clearly be seen through the window without any unnecessary peeping.

As I stood there stunned, I thought: "That's what they look like!" I had never seen a live naked female except my little sister. I can remember going home in shock, avoiding my mother's eyes because I knew that she could look at me and know that I had seen a live naked girl. I can remember the funny feeling I got every time I walked past that building. In time I got over it but it was a real shock for me at that time in life.

My, how things have changed! Kids in Jr. High school are exposed to more sexual stimuli than the previous generations were and as a result it is necessary to discuss the impact that the exposure will have on them. The newspapers carry the stories everyday of younger and younger girls having babies and young boys boasting of their sexual powers. The result is a lackadaisical, ho-hum attitude about the dangers of sex and very few people taking seriously the damaging effect of the sexual stimuli that young people are exposed to.

As a result of all of the sexual exposure it becomes difficult to look at a beautiful woman and not take her clothes off in your mind. This puts the man in prison. Any man or woman who cannot look at someone of the opposite sex without undressing them in their mind is in PRISON!

The mind must be free and you will need to fight to keep it free. THE MIND IS THE MOST IMPORTANT SEX ORGAN. So, the question then becomes: "How can I think pure thoughts when I encounter that gorgeous creature of the opposite sex?

I would like to equip you with some thoughts that will help you gain the victory in this area of life.

1. TELL YOURSELF THAT THE GORGEOUS BODY THAT YOU ARE LOOKING AT ALSO HAS A SOUL AND SPIRIT.

The spirit of this person hangs out with God and He is always closer to her than you will ever get to be. When you do this you remind yourself that the woman is an eternal creature who will exist in spirit form for an eternity. Any woman's relationship with a man is temporary but her relationship with God is eternal.

> *What! know ye not that your body is the temple of the Holy Ghost which is in you, which ye have of God, and ye are not your own? For ye are bought with a price: therefore glorify God in your body, and in your spirit, which are God's.*
>
> *I Corinthians 6:19-20*

2. TELL YOURSELF THAT THE WOMAN THAT YOU ARE LOOKING AT HAS A FAMILY.

She may have a father, brother, and family members that love her as a daughter, sister, or cousin. It is always a family affair when you get involved with a woman because families generally protect their women and women love their families. The goal is to respect the woman in your mind as well as with your actions. God judges not only your actions but He is concerned about your thoughts.

> *But I say unto you, That whosoever looketh on a woman to lust after her hath committed adultery with her already in his heart.*
>
> *Matthew 5:28*

> *(Treat) The elder women as mothers; the younger as sisters, with all purity.*
>
> *I Timothy 5:2*

3. TELL YOURSELF THAT THE WOMAN THAT YOU ARE LOOKING AT HAS GOALS, DREAMS AND A MIND OF HER OWN.

It is amazing to talk to a woman sometimes and see where her head is. A man is thinking about her body and she is thinking something totally different.

4. CONSIDER THE FACT THAT ALTHOUGH SHE IS PRETTY, SHE MAY HAVE MEDICAL PROBLEMS.

The female body is an amazing thing with many complicated parts. A woman has many things to deal with that men don't know anything about. You will learn more about this when you marry and live with a woman.

5. REALIZE THAT THE PERSONALITY AND REAL CHARACTER OF THE WOMAN MAY NOT MATCH HER PRETTY FACE.

I know of a young lady who was so pretty that when she walked into a room that every male head turned in her direction. She knew that she was pretty and she enjoyed all of the attention that she received. What was unfortunate about her situation was that she allowed it to go to her head and her personality was terrible.

I know many men who hooked up with beautiful women just for their beauty and shortly after the beginning of their marriage or relationship they found out that they were very miserable. Remember that a pretty face can hide an empty mind.

6. DETERMINE TO WHAT DEGREE YOU CHOOSE TO BE CONTROLLED BY LUSTFUL THOUGHTS AND FEMALES IN GENERAL.

I stopped in a convenient store to get some gas. As I went inside to pay, there was a women standing at the counter with some beautiful legs and shorts on that were cut very high. Standing behind her in line were four men and I made the fifth. As I stood there I noticed that there was much tension in the air because all of the men standing behind her were nervous. All of them could see her legs but none of them wanted to act like they were bothered by them. As the lady paid for her gas and left all of the men's heads took a last peek at the legs that carried her to her car.

After she left, the men in the store sighed a sigh of relief. I said to the man in front of me: "She had some pretty legs didn't she" He looked at me, shook his head and said: **"SURE DID!"** What I find interesting about this situation was the manner in which the men handled being in the presence of these pretty legs. There was a tenseness in the air because of the presence of this woman and how the men allowed themselves to be impacted by her. When this happens to you, this is what you do. Acknowledge to yourself or another man that the woman is pretty. When you do this you release the pressure that is going on in your mind.

This defuses many of the additional negative thoughts that would occur if the situation were not faced head on. This also allows you to be at peace with yourself because you are not fighting the negative thoughts that occur when you have secret sexual fantasies in your mind.

Somehow in our culture it has become an acceptable behavior for a man to be out of control in the presence of a pretty woman. TV and movies make it appear that men have no control over the matter. **This is not the case!** You can CHOOSE to what degree you want to allow a woman's beauty to manipulate you.

> *I made a covenant with mine eyes; why then should I think upon a maid?*
>
> *Job 31:1*

I challenge you do to like Job did, he made an agreement with his eyes. Many men need to do this today.

QUESTIONS
FOR INTROSPECTION AND DISCUSSION
(to make you think)

1. What do you think when a pretty young woman sits next to you?_____

2. Do you challenge negative sexual thoughts about women or do you let your mind run wild_____

3. Do you have a pretty sister?_____

4. Who do you talk to about women or what source provides you with your information about women?_____

5. Have you considered the fact that if the Lord lets you live you will be older one day and sex will not be a priority in your life?_____

APPLICABLE SCRIPTURES

Lust not after her beauty in thine heart; neither let her take thee with her eyelids. For by means of a whorish woman a man is brought to a piece of bread: and the adultress will hunt for the precious life.

Proverbs 6:25-26

But I say unto you, That whosoever looketh on a woman to lust after hath committed adultery with her already in his heart.

Matthew 5:28

And it came to pass in an eveningtide, that David arose from off his bed, and walked upon the roof of the king's house: and from the roof he saw a woman washing herself; and the woman was very beautiful to look upon.

II Samuel 11:2

But every man is tempted, when he is drawn away of his own lust, and enticed.

James 1:14

But if they cannot contain, let them marry: for it is better to marry than to burn.

I Corinthians 7:9

> *I beseech you therefore, brethren, by the mercies of God, that ye present your bodies a living sacrifice, holy, acceptable unto god, which is your reasonable service. And be not conformed to this world: but be ye transformed by the renewing of your mind, that ye may prove what is that good, and acceptable, and perfect, will of God.*
>
> *Romans 12:1-2*

Notes:_____

_____

_____

_____

_____

_____

_____

PART FIVE

WHO'S IN CHARGE?

CHAPTER EIGHTEEN

Who Is Your Judge ?

EVERY YOUNG MAN NEEDS A JUDGE. Usually a father fills this role. A very fortunate young man will have many men in his life who judge him from time to time. Isaiah 1:23 talks about the Jews who are about to be destroyed. Listen to what he says: *"Thy princes are rebellious, and companions of thieves: every one loveth gifts, and followeth after rewards: they judge not the fatherless, neither doth the cause of the widow come unto them."*

CONSEQUENCES OF NOT HAVING JUDGES

This Scripture speaks about the consequences of not having judges. When the men of a society stop caring for, correcting, and instructing the young of that society (even though the children are not biologically theirs), destruction is just up the road. So, I ask the young man a question. Who are your judges? And I ask the mature Black man: "What young man are you judging?" When we speak of a judge, we are speaking of a mature older person who can provide guidance and correction.

A youth without a man to respect and receive guidance and correction from will find life difficult. No matter how gifted and talented he may be, the road will be rough if a young man is too free. A Judge to call him out when he is wrong will provide guidance for a young man and help him live longer.

WHO ARE THE BEST POSSIBLE JUDGES?

A judge may be a coach, teacher, uncle, pastor, boss, counsellor or any man who genuinely cares for you and seeks your best good. Be sure to consider the role that God plays in his life. People who love God are far from perfect but you at least know where they are trying to come from.

HOW TO GET THE MOST FROM YOUR JUDGES.

People enjoy the opportunity to reproduce themselves. A man receives gratification from a son who follows in his footsteps. Most mature men would be flattered for you to ask them to participate in the process of molding you into a man. So, you need to show an older man that you have these qualities:

•**DESIRE** - Express your desire to be tutored, discipled and taught by the older man.
•**PATIENCE** - Once you've expressed that desire, don't rush him. Even mature men have their hands full keeping their own lives together. Be patient.
•**SUBMISSION** - Be prepared to submit and do some things you don't want to do or don't make a lot of sense to you. Think about it, if it made sense to you, you wouldn't need the older wiser man to tell you to do it.
•**TRANSPARENCY** - Be transparent with the older man. Don't hide your feelings. He was young once and knows what it is like.
•**ZEAL** - Anything he asks you to do, do it well.

Seek you out a wise man. Apart from kin folk, your pastor should be one of your main judges. The reason is that a good pastor loves you and God will work through your pastor to instruct you. This method is safe and I recommend it.

> *Where no counsel is, the people fall: but in the multitude of counsellors there is safety.*
> *Proverbs 11:14*

QUESTIONS
FOR INTROSPECTION OR DISCUSSION
(to make you think)

1. How many good mature men are you subject to? List them.

   _____

   _____

   _____

2. Do they know you feel this way? _____

3. Do you have the discipline to do what they say? _____

4. Can you think of a time when an older wiser man asked you to do something, you refused to do it, and later found out that he was right? Discuss or think about it. Ask yourself questions and learn how to benefit from a similar situation when it happens in the future.

   _____

   _____

5. Have you ever been to court and submitted to a Judge on the bench? ___Yes___No. How did it feel? _____

6. Do you see the advantage of getting a judge who will guide you in a manner that will keep you away from the judge on the bench? ___Yes ___No

APPLICABLE SCRIPTURES

A wise man will hear, and will increase learning; and a man of understanding shall attain unto wise counsels:

Proverbs 1:5

Turn you at my reproof: behold, I will pour out my spirit unto you, I will make known my words unto you.

Proverbs 1:23

My son, despise not the chastening of the LORD; neither be weary of his correction: For whom the Lord loveth he correcteth; even as a father the son in whom he delighteth.

Proverbs 3:11,12

Hear, O my son, and receive my sayings; and the years of thy life shall be many.

Proverbs 4:10

CHAPTER NINETEEN

The Principle Of Authority

WHEN I WAS 18 YEARS OLD, I HAD A younger brother who was 2 years old. He was the first toddler that I encountered as a adult. I found his development very interesting, especially his first words. His favorite first words were: "Don't tell me!" He was in his own world, doing his own thing and when you sought to guide or interact with him he would say: "Don't tell me!" At times he would even put his hands over his ears, look away and say: "DON'T TELL ME!"

At the time I would think that the kid was trippin' and I would ignore him. I have since learned that what he was doing was quite natural because the Bible teaches that we are born in a state of rebellion. We are born rebelling against anybody who puts restraints on us. King David knew this when he said:

Behold, I was shapen in iniquity; and in sin did my mother conceive me.
Psalm 51:5

The wicked are estranged from the womb: they go astray as soon as they be born, speaking lies.
Psalm 58:3

There was a time in my life when I had a problem with the concept of being born a sinner. And then I had kids. Each child said "da da" first, because it was easy to say. The second word was "NO!"

Because of the theological truth that we are born in

sin, it becomes necessary for us to be born again which frees us from the slavery of sin. Once we are born again we no longer need to be slaves to passion, greed, anger, violence, girls, or any other thing.

With this in mind, we look at the principle of authority. One of the most difficult things for a man or woman to do is to submit to authority. Part of the reason we reject authority is due to our nature. Another reason is because of our culture. We have already discussed our nature, so let's look at our culture.

We have a culture that is very prideful. The media appeals to our pride in it's programming and commercials. People are encouraged to do things to get even and vindicate themselves when 'dissed' or insulted. We see that pride is rampant in our society.

With all of the emphasis on pride, the principle of authority suffers. Regardless of what men think, God has said that we all need authority in our lives. One of the classic Scriptures on this subject is I Corinthians 11:3.

> *But I would have you know, that the head of every man is Christ; and the head of the woman is the man; and the head of Christ is God.*
>
> *I Corinthians 11:3*

It is clear from Scripture and from observation that a young man who learns that there are people in his life that can tell him what to do will go further than the young man who rebels against authority. Let's list examples of authority figures in our lives: Parents, Teachers, Preachers, Deans, Principals, Police, Employers, Mayors, Governors, Presidents and God, just to name a few.

Now, what most young Black men don't understand is that there is a progression of authority in their lives. When you come into conflict with one of them you are in conflict with ALL of them! Let me explain. When you fall out with the Teacher, she calls the Dean. When you fall out with the Dean, he calls the Principal. When you fall out with the Principal, he calls the Police who escort you off of campus and it goes on and on and on.

So, the wise thing is to realize that WHEN YOU DEAL WITH ONE AUTHORITY FIGURE, YOU DEAL WITH THEM ALL! A police officer told me that when a Black male puffs his chest and resists his authority, he simply calls for back up.

The wise brother will deal with all authority figures in such a manner that they will not send him to the next level.

A wise young man will seek to win the favor of those in authority in his life. This does not mean that you have to kiss their toes, but it does men that you should be kind to them. In most cases, they will respond in kindness. If they are mean to you, be pleasant to them anyway and God will bless you in spite of their attitude.

If you are lazy, evil, wrong, trippin' or acting inappropriately, it is the job of the authority figures in your life to make you get yourself together. It amazes me how some people can be as wrong as two left feet and complain when someone corrects them.

QUESTIONS
FOR DISCUSSION AND INTROSPECTION
(to make you think)

1. What authority figure do you have the biggest problem with?_____

2. When was the last time you were mistreated by an authority figure?_____
How did you respond?_____

3. Do you ever feel rebellious for no apparent reason?

_____ _____

4. Do you listen to music or RAP that encourages rebellion?
___ Yes ___ No

5. What concrete steps are you taking to help you deal with the authority in your life?_____

APPLICABLE SCRIPTURES

Let every soul be subject unto the higher powers. For there is no power but of God: the powers that be are ordained of God. Whosoever therefore resisteth the power, resisteth the ordinance of God: and they that resist shall receive to themselves damnation. For rulers are not a terror to good works, but to the evil. Wilt thou then not be afraid of the power? Do that which is good, and thou shalt have praise of the same:

Romans 13:1-3

It is an abomination to kings to commit wickedness: for the throne is established by righteousness.

Proverbs 16:12

Hear counsel, and receive instruction, that thou mayest be wise in thy latter end.

Proverbs 19:20

The king's heart is in the hand of the LORD, as the rivers of water: he turneth it withersoever he will.

Proverbs 21:1

He that hath no rule over his own spirit is like a city that is broken down, and without walls.

Proverbs 25:28

Notes:_____

_____

_____

_____

_____

_____

_____

_____

_____

_____

CHAPTER TWENTY

IS IT REALLY NECESSARY TO CURSE????

I WAS IN THE MALL THE OTHER DAY AND there was a basketball court set up for a promotion. People were invited to take some shots for prizes. I must say that I was embarrassed at some brothers there who were foul. In a crowded mall they were talking like this: "Yo man, what the *&^% &6%^&<, *$#&, you doin? You can't make no *&%^, ^%$&, $#% shots!" Not only were they using profanity, they were also very loud.

When you curse in public you only show that you:
- Have a limited vocabulary.
- Have not been properly trained. (no home trainin')
- Don't respect those who are offended by profanity.
- Don't respect yourself and the other Black men who will be looked upon negatively because of your behavior.
- Are probably not a person that people will want to get to know.

Profanity impresses no one but you. For some strange reason the person who curses believes that something positive is being accomplished through his negative behavior.

If you are one who is prone to foul language you need to consider several things:
- Your motivation for cursing.
- Your understanding of cursing.
- How you are perceived because of your cursing.
- What you can do to stop cursing.

Lets consider your motivation for cursing.

All behavior is motivated by something. If you are prone to profanity, there is a reason why you continue to do it. In most cases, it is because you grew up around it and found it to be the language spoken in your environment. If this is the case, you need to do what was stated in chapter one where we discussed dealing with your orientation. If you curse because you are pressured by those around you, then you need to get a grip. This type of response to peer pressure is an indication that you have a weak personality. If your motivation is it makes you feel big or powerful, this is a misbelief because the opposite is true.

Let's look at your understanding of cursing.

I was in the presence of an elderly gentleman who was angry and he was cursing. He was so old that he had one foot in the grave and the other on a banana peel. As a pastor I went to him and gently reminded him that he shouldn't curse. He looked at me angrily and said: "I ain't cursing, only God can curse somebody." I thought about what he said and he was right.

When you curse what you are really doing is asking God to place His displeasure and condemnation on something or someone. When you say: "Damn It! or Damn You" you are actually asking God to condemn that person or thing to Hell! If God were listening to you the people you cursed would be in big trouble. The fact of the matter is that when you curse, God does not listen to you, he laughs at you.

Why do the heathen rage, and the people imagine a vain thing? He that sitteth in the heavens shall laugh: the LORD shall have them in derision.
Psalm 2:1,4

Cursing really makes a mockery of God and the fact that people who reject Him will actually be damned because they refused the free gift of salvation. It is a dangerous thing to play with God by cursing.

Let's consider how you are perceived because of your cursing:

When you curse around other people who curse, you fit in. If fitting in is your major goal in life then it will be necessary for you to curse for the rest of your life. Fitting in around those who curse is not what I consider to be a progressive attitude and approach to life. Cursing appeals to the wrong crowd. I suggest that you choose to appeal to the crowd that rejects this lifestyle and attitude.

Let's consider how to stop if you have started cursing.
1. Start with a realization that God is displeased by the behavior.

> *I call heaven and earth to record this day against you, that I have set before you life and death, blessing and cursing: therefore choose life, that both thou and thy seed may live:*
>
> *Deuteronomy 30:19*

God's design for us is a pure heart and clean lips. The fact that you are angry is not an issue with God.

2. Realize that you will hear all of your words again when you stand before God in judgment.

> *But I say unto you, That every idle word that men shall speak, they shall give account thereof in the day of judgment. For by thy words thou shalt be justified, and by thy words thou shalt be condemned.*
>
> *Matthew 12:36-37*

The Bible clearly teaches that not one word that comes out of your mouth will go unnoticed by God. The book of Revelation teaches that God has a book and He has many books. These books contain the deeds of all mankind. It is for this reason that the Christian believes that evil words and deeds will not go unpunished.

> *And I saw the dead, small and great, stand before God; and the books were opened: and another book was opened, which is the book of life: and the dead were judged out of those things which were written in the books, according to their works.*
>
> *Revelation 20:12*

3. Ask God to give you a disdain for profanity.

> *Create in me a clean heart, O God; and renew a right spirit within me.*
>
> *Psalm 51:10*

I am amazed at the men I know personally whom God has touched and changed. God can clean your heart which will result in a clean tongue.

> *A wholesome tongue is a tree of life: but perverseness therein is a breach in the spirit.*
>
> *Proverbs 15:4*

4. Tell some person that you hang with that you are trying to stop cursing.

> *Confess your faults one to another, and pray one for another, that ye may be healed. The effectual fervent prayer of a righteous man availeth much.*
>> *James 5:16*

There is power in open confession before God and friends who want to help you overcome your weakness. Always strive to hang with people who will hold you accountable. This may require that you find some new friends who will agree with your new direction in life. It is OK and advised to leave old friends who are not a good influence.

5. Work to replace curse words with new powerful words that will express your feelings and emotions in the place of the curse words.

> *The tongue of the wise useth knowledge aright: but the mouth of fools poureth out foolishness.*
>> *Proverbs 15:2*

> *The Lord God hath given me the tongue of the learned, that I should know how to speak a word in season to him that is weary: he wakeneth morning by morning, he wakeneth mine ear to hear as the learned.*
>> *Isaiah 50:4*

A desire to express disgust, anger or disappointment in the most emphatic way can be communicated through words other than curse words. To adequately express your emotions is another reason to enhance your vocabulary.

QUESTIONS
FOR INTROSPECTION AND DISCUSSION
(to make you think)

1. Do you curse?   Yes____ No____

2. Do you come from a cursing environment? Yes____ No____

3. Give your reason for cursing or not cursing_____

4. What is your perception of those who curse?_____
   _____

5. Do you really believe that God is concerned about what comes out of your mouth? Yes____ No____

6. Do you believe that there will be a future judgment for your words and deeds? Yes____ No____

7. Are you committed to increasing your vocabulary?
   Yes____   No____

APPLICABLE SCRIPTURES

> *Thou art snared with the words of thy mouth, thou art taken with the words of thy mouth.*
>
> *Proverbs 6:2*

> *For my mouth shall speak truth; and wickedness is an abomination to my lips.*
>
> *Proverbs 8:7*

The lips of the righteous feed many: but fools die for want of wisdom.

Proverbs 10:21

The lips of the righteous know what is acceptable: but the mouth of the wicked speaketh frowardness.

Proverbs 10:32

Lying lips are abomination to the LORD: but they that deal truly are his delight.

Proverbs 12:22

He that keepeth his mouth keepeth his life: but he that openeth wide his lips shall have destruction.

Proverbs 13:3

The tongue of the wise useth knowledge aright: but the mouth of fools poureth out foolishness.

Proverbs 15:2

A wholesome tongue is a tree of life: but perverseness therein is a breach in the spirit.

Proverbs 15:4

Righteous lips are the delight of kings; and they love him that speaketh right.

Proverbs 16:13

Even a fool, when he holdeth his peace, is counted wise: and he that shutteth his lips is esteemed a man of understanding.

Proverbs 17:28

Notes:_____

_____

_____

_____

_____

_____

_____

_____

_____

_____

CHAPTER TWENTY ONE

How Grown Is Grown?

A STRONG POINT OF CONTENTION FOR children and their parents is the subject of maturity. The reason there is tension in this area is becausethe child and the parent have different opinions about how mature the child is. See if this sounds familiar.

Parent: "You can't stay out past 11:00!"
Child: "Aw Momma!, I know how to watch myself!"
Parent "You are too young to date!"
Child: "Other kids my age are already dating!"
Parent: "Don't take the car on the interstate!"
Child: "I can drive on the interstate as good as you can!"

These are a few examples of typical discussions that parents have with their young men. I often tell young men to be patient with their parents as they struggle to let them grow up. I also tell parents to be careful not to hold on to their young men too tightly (especially mothers).

My sixteenth birthday was one of the greatest days of my life. I had been waiting for years to be able to get behind the wheel of a car legally. I didn't sleep much the night before. The next day, I was up early and on the bus to the drivers license place. After becoming a legal driver, I was made aware of the responsibilities that came with the license.

I was now sinking all of my money into a raggedy hoopty (car) that ran some of the time. I now received requests from friends and family to take them places. It became difficult to tell the difference between those who liked me and those who liked my car. After a while, the car was no big deal, just a means to get from point "A" to point

"B". When considering the subject of maturity, there are some points you should keep in mind:

1. YOU ARE CONSTANTLY REACHING NEW LEVELS OF MATURITY.

Growth is one of the most exciting aspects of living. The maturing process is one in which you understand today what you couldn't understand yesterday. It is amazing that at certain ages it is impossible for the average brain to understand and process certain information. This is why in school you learn to spell, read, add, multiply, divide, do decimals at the age when the mind is able to handle it. Just as this is true in school, it is true in life. There are certain things you cannot understand until you reach a level of maturity that comprehends these concepts. I think that this concept is easy to understand when you look back to the past and see how you have grown in your understanding of the world around you. When you do look back and examine the past, you will see that you are reaching new levels of maturity.

2. REMEMBER THAT NO MATTER WHERE YOU ARE ON THE MATURITY SCALE TODAY, YOU WILL CHANGE.

Most people become more mature as time passes. With this in mind, you should realize that your points of reference and your values will change. Your understanding of what is important to you in high school will change when you get in college. Your understanding of what is important in college will change when you graduate and get married. Once you have children, everything changes again.

Most men look back and wish they had made some different decisions back in Jr. High School, like: studying more, not wasting time, not experimenting with drugs, not taking some of the chances they took, realizing that they should have listened to Mrs. Thompson, Dean Smith and Coach Russell. With this fact in mind, most men look back and wish they had made wiser, more mature decisions when they were young. It would be wise for young men to seek wisdom when making decisions while in Jr. High School, High School, College and beyond. You are going to change when it comes to the maturity used in making decisions.

One common regret that many men have later in life is in the area of education. Many men regret not studying more! Because of their current level of maturity, they see the benefit of studying and staying in school. Remember that no matter where you are on the maturity scale today, you will change.

3. YOU DON'T AUTOMATICALLY GET WISER WITH AGE.

Wisdom and understanding which are the ingredients for growth are missing from many young men today. The reason for this is that they are not getting wisdom. YOU WILL NEVER BE SAFELY GROWN UNTIL YOU GET WISDOM! Wisdom is something that you GET. It must be obtained and does not come naturally. It comes when young men rub shoulders with older wiser men and God.

Wisdom allows you to see the bigger picture. Men without wisdom only see the immediate situation. A man without wisdom will go to bed with a girl not considering the long term consequences. A man without wisdom will walk out of school because he cannot overlook one incident that made him mad.

Wisdom is different from knowledge because wisdom tells you when to use your knowledge. A man who has knowledge without wisdom is an educated fool. One of the best sources of wisdom that I know about is the Book of Proverbs which is found in the middle of your Bible. I meditate on one chapter of Proverbs a week, reading it each morning and I have found it a great source of wisdom. Remember, you don't automatically get wiser with age.

YOU WILL NEVER BE SAFELY GROWN UNTIL YOU GET WISDOM!

4. AVOID THE PERSON WHO CLAIMS TO HAVE THE MATURITY THING ALL TOGETHER.

The maturity process is like standing on the edge of a cliff. You must constantly work hard to balance yourself or you may have a big accident. The person who claims to have it all together is either lying or they are not aware of the world around them. There is a danger in being impressed with other who seem to be so cool and handle their problems with ease. Any person who will be honest with you will admit that he needs more wisdom sometimes. There are days when I use all the wisdom that I have trying to deal with my problem for that day. Any person who will not admit to that fact is lying.

Sufficient unto the day is the evil thereof.
Matthew 6:34b

This is one of the ways that God grows us. He takes us to the outer, raw, frightening limits of our understanding with a problem. While in this condition and position we see that we are inadequate. God then provides us with additional wisdom through His Spirit, His Word, His man or through some part of His creation. When this process takes place we are growing and becoming more mature. So, avoid the person who claims to have the maturity thing all together.

5. CONSIDER YOUR SUBSIDIZATION

To be subsidized is to be supported financially. It is the responsibility of the parents to protect and provide for their children. As long as you live in your parent's house, and are subsidized by them, you are not grown. You may be old, but you are not grown. One of the necessary lessons for maturity is what you learn when you provide for yourself.

When you get out on your own, you get a perspective that you have never had before. Not only does this help you grow up, it enables your parent(s) to experience an empty home which is part of their maturity process. My mother recently had the experience of the last child leaving. She now has the freedom to go and come as she pleases, take trips and enjoy life. This is a freedom that your parents deserve.

I challenge you to realize that no matter how grown you think you are, there is a lot of growing to do in each area of life. I also challenge you to be a sponge around those with wisdom, be willing to step up to new levels of maturity and accept new challenges. Finally, I challenge you to be gracious and kind with your wisdom. It was given to you so never look down on those with less wisdom than you have.

QUESTIONS
FOR INTROSPECTION AND DISCUSSION
(to make you think)

1. Do you consider yourself smart for your age?
   Yes___No___

2. Do you consider yourself wise for your age?
   Yes___No___

3. Can you accept a wise statement before you fully understand it? If an older wise man shares wisdom with you, do you reject it if you have not experienced it? Yes___No___

4. When was the last time you thought you were grown and found out (the hard way) that you were not grown? (explain)

_____

5. Using a scale of 1 to 10 with 10 being the highest, rate your maturity in these areas:

> Maturity with girls:
> 1 2 3 4 5 6 7 8 9 10
> Maturity in staying away from drugs, gangs, and evil people:
> 1 2 3 4 5 6 7 8 9 10
> Maturity with money:
> 1 2 3 4 5 6 7 8 9 10
> Maturity in understanding and relating to adults:
> 1 2 3 4 5 6 7 8 9 10
> Maturity regarding your education:
> 1 2 3 4 5 6 7 8 9 10

6. Rate your maturity in these same areas two years ago.
Girls
1 2 3 4 5 6 7 8 9 10
Staying away form drugs, gangs, and evil people
1 2 3 4 5 6 7 8 9 10
Money
1 2 3 4 5 6 7 8 9 10
Relating to adults
1 2 3 4 5 6 7 8 9 10

Regarding your education
1 2 3 4 5 6 7 8 9 10

7. Name five specific things that you are doing to get more wisdom.

    1. _____

    2. _____

    3._____

    4._____

    5._____

8. As a result of this lesson, will you realize that maturity or being grown is not a magic number like 16,18, or 21? However it is a life long process of acquiring wisdom and applying it in each decision we make.

APPLICABLE SCRIPTURES

My son, hear the instruction of thy father, and forsake not the law of thy mother: For they shall be an ornament of grace unto thy head, and chains about thy neck.

Proverbs 1:8-9

Trust in the Lord with all thine heart; and lean not unto thine own understanding.

Proverbs 3:5

Better is a poor and wise child than an old and foolish king, who will no more be admonished.

Ecclesiastes 4:13

Wisdom strengtheneth the wise more than ten mighty men which are in the city.

Ecclesiastes 7:19

If any of you lack wisdom, let him ask of God, that giveth to all men liberally, and upbraideth not; and it shall be given him.

James 1:5

Children, obey your parents in the Lord: for this is right.

Ephesians 6:1

When I was a child, I spake as a child, I understood as a child, I thought as a child: but when I became a man, I put away childish things.

I Corinthians 13:11

PART SIX

FRIEND OR FOE?

CHAPTER TWENTY TWO

Understanding The White Man

THE REAL DEAL WITH THE WHITE MAN IS that he is scared. He is scared about the economy, the fact that his kids may be on drugs and that his wife may divorce him. He is afraid that his life as he has known it for many years will change.

Please note that there are two types of White men:
•The type that trusts in his own strength and ingenuity, or the self- contained White man.
•The type that trusts God for his future, or the Christ-contained White man.

The type of White man that we need to be concerned about is the one who trusts in himself and his money. Because of the browning of America, this man has to face a level of competition that he has never had to deal with before. The self contained White man lives in the midst of a changing world that he can't control. Because of this, he is frustrated. The apostle Paul described this man like this.

Whose end is destruction, whose God is their belly, and whose glory is in their shame, who mind earthly things.

Philippians 3:19

When you add to these conditions that the White race has suffered from a decline in Godly men just as the Black race has, you can see why it is so easy for unspiritual White men to blame others for their situation.

One thing that most men hate is change. We are all creatures of habit and change threatens us. Resistance to the

Civil Rights movement in the United States was fueled in part by a fear of change. We can see the struggle in our government over what should and shouldn't change. So, the real deal with the White man is that he does not want things to change much.

As I said earlier, White men are scared. The media perpetuates the fear. Each evening on the news they see Black men committing crimes against helpless victims. Consequently, when they meet a Black male who looks like those seen on TV, common sense tells him to beware.

For those Black men who have had the opportunity to develop good friendships with White men who are educationally and economically similar, they learn that the difference between Black and White men are cosmetic and cultural. Close interracial friends soon learn that they struggle with the same things. The major differences between Black and White are those which come as a result of economic and educational opportunities.

One of the greatest challenges that Black and White men face is the challenge of giving each other the opportunity to evaluate each other on the basis of the individual's character as opposed to the way one looks.

The problem is that it is not that simple. You cannot judge a book by its cover. I work with youth and I occasionally dress like a man much younger than I actually am. When I dress in jeans and tennis shoes, it is very common for me to be followed around in the mall by the security staff. Yes, that's right, the Reverend Doctor Harold Davis who is on the pastoral staff of Canaan Missionary Baptist Church is followed around in the mall when he dresses a certain way. The reason this happens is that people are scared and they will judge you based on how you look.

This is a terrible reality that Black and White people must realize. I am not as hard on White people, as I used to be. When they are suspicious of me based on how I look. I am a member of a predominantly Black Church with a few very faithful and loving White members. Not too long ago, a young White Christian brother and his friend cut off all of their hair and came to Bible study. They sat on the far side of the Church. From where I sat, I had difficulty seeing who they were with all of their hair cut off.

As I looked at the two unknown White men with all of the "skin" showing on the top of their heads, I was initially uncomfortable. They reminded me of the racist, violent 'skin heads' who were gaining popularity. After service, when I was able to get close enough to see who it was, I realized that I, just like White people could jump to conclusions, based on what could be seen.

Ignorance of individuals or ignorance of groups of individuals fosters fear. And then again, we all know that there are some people who are just ignorant and have decided to hate people that are different than they are. Listen to what king David prayed concerning these men:

Deliver me, O LORD, from the evil man: preserve me from the violent man; Which imagine mischiefs in their heart continually are they gathered together for war. They have sharpened their tongues like a serpent; adders' poison is under their lips. Selah. Keep me, O LORD, from the hands of the wicked; preserve me from the violent man; who have purposed to overthrow my goings.

Psalms 140:1-4

I am convinced based on the Bible and history that those who hate without cause will be rewarded with evil on earth and also in the world to come. Freedom comes when a man frees his heart from malice or hate. Well, the current situation calls for a strategy that will guide our actions as we come into contact with White men. This strategy should include the following characteristics:

• You must be fair to the stranger.

• You must be able to have a clear conscious before God after each meeting or interaction with a White man.

1. APPROACH THE INDIVIDUAL FROM THE POSITION OF STRENGTH.

Realize that God is with you because you are not prejudging the individual but extending to him basic human and Christian kindness. Your response to his response will depend on your level of maturity.

2. IF HE RESPONDS WITH KINDNESS EQUAL TO YOUR LEVEL OF KINDNESS YOU KNOW THAT YOU ARE DEALING WITH A REASONABLE PERSON AND YOU MAY PROCEED TO GET TO KNOW THE MAN BETTER.

3. IF HE RESPONDS WITH ANY DEGREE OF HOSTILITY YOU MAY CHOOSE TO MOVE ON TO AVOID ENDANGERING EITHER MAN'S DELICATE EGO WHICH COULD RESULT IN WORDS OR WEAPONS.

If you are in a situation where you must be around this person (school, work, army, etc.) you must first of all protect yourself by dotting your "i's" and crossing your "t's." From that point you must decide which of the following options you wish to take.

Option A:

This is the best option which involves letting Jesus use you as an instrument of HIS peace. By this I mean that Jesus wants to love this person through you and possibly win a White man to salvation through the efforts of a Black man. When this happens, a spontaneous party of praise breaks out in heaven which is so severe that it takes several minutes for the place to settle down. Interracial witnessing and winning of people to Christ is a tremendous example to those who are watching and they are stretched to believe in God.

I have had the opportunity to witness to many White men and have had the privilege of winning some to Christ. I did this in some cases when they were not totally cordial, courteous or kind to me. I can tell you that the experience has made me a better, wiser, more mature man who has reaped personal benefits from option "A".

Option B:

This option involves you extending kindness to the man even though he is rude to you. God promises that when you do this it drives the man crazy!

> *Therefore if thine enemy hunger, feed him; if he thirst, give him drink: for in so doing thou shalt heap coals of fire on his head.*
>
> *Romans 12:20*

Remember, regardless of how he responds you will be blessed by acting like Jesus would act.

Option C:

This option is the least desirable which would involve extending no love to the man, just existing together while you must be there. This is the option that many Americans, Black and White are taking and it is unfortunate. If you are a Christian, a man who is secure in himself, God expects more. If you are not a Christian, I don't see any way possible to be kind to a racist White person (remember Dr. King). This fair strategy will guide you as you meet the White man each day.

When dealing with a White man, always try to determine if he is self contained or Christ contained. As a Black man, don't allow yourself to fall into the narrow line of thinking which puts forth the idea that ALL White men are bad. History shows that good White men have stood side by side with Black men from the beginning of the civil rights movement even to today. In my own life I can remember many Christ contained White men assisting my father as he struggled to feed his large family.

When I stop and look at the world, I notice that White men are fighting White men in the old Soviet Republics, Koreans are fighting Koreans in Korea, Africans are fighting Africans in Africa. When you study the conflicts in the world, it is plain to see that the source of conflict is not based on man's color but it is based on who contains the man. The source of all conflict among men is religious in nature. We know that in the end, man will be divided based on his religion.

So, in order to understand the White man, resolve to get to know him well enough to see who contains him. If he is self-contained, greed will motivate him and his motto will be to "Do unto others before they do unto you." If he is Christ-contained his motto will be to "Do unto others as you would have them do unto you."

Pray that God will give you the discernment and wisdom to be sensitive to every man's heart and quick to discern who contains each man you meet.

QUESTIONS
FOR INTROSPECTION OR DISCUSSION
(to make you think)

1. Tell the truth, shame the devil! Are you prejudice?_____

2. If you are, have you analyzed why you are?_____

3. Do you understand how that prejudice and hatred only hurt you?_____

4. What White man have you had problems with (because of the color of your skin) and how have you dealt with the situation?_____

5. What are you doing to combat the negative images that Black males have through the media?_____

   _____

6. Which option do you most frequently use in dealing with White men: Option A, B, or C_____

7. If you are not using Option "A", do you desire to grow to the point where you can use that option on a regular basis? ___Yes ___ No

8. All men are contained by someone. Who contains you?

   _____

APPLICABLE SCRIPTURES

He that saith he is in the light, and hateth his brother, is in darkness even until now.

I John 2:9

For there is no difference between the Jew and the Greek: for the same Lord over all is rich unto all that call upon him.

Romans 10:12

There is neither Jew nor Greek, there is neither bond nor free, there is neither male nor female: for ye are all one in Christ Jesus.

Galatians 3:28

Let all bitterness, and wrath, and anger, and clamor, and evil speaking, be put away from you, with all malice:

Ephesians 4:31

Brethren, be not children in understanding: howbeit in malice be ye children, but in understanding be men.

I Corinthians 14:20

But evil men and seducers shall wax worse and worse, deceiving, and being deceived.

II Timothy 3:13

Owe no man any thing, but to love one another: for he that loveth another hath fulfilled the law.

Romans 13:8

CHAPTER TWENTY THREE

Cops And Robbers

ONE OF THE GREAT CHALLENGES FACING young Black men is the legal system with the local police department in particular. Not long ago I was going to a friend's house to pick up my son. As I neared his house I noticed four police cars up the street. I went around the block to avoid the scene and passed one police car in the process. As I parked my car and got out, a policeman approached me and told me to stand still. The thought that first went through my mind was: "What does he want?" The second thought was that I don't like being told what to do. The third thought was be cool and remember Rodney King. As the officer approached me, I purposely maintained an attitude and posture of confidence (not arrogance).

The officer and I talked and I was very pleasant with him and treated him with all of the respect that his uniform deserved. He informed me that there had been an altercation (fight) up the street and one of the men had on a red shirt (I had on a red shirt) and blue pants (I had on blue pants). After talking with me very briefly the officer determined that I was not the person that he was looking for and APOLOGIZED and went his way.

One of the joys of getting older is you learn how to handle potentially dangerous situations. You develop a perspective that is broader than your own interests. You learn to see the other side of the picture. When it comes to law enforcement the young Black male needs to be objectively taught how to handle themselves around policemen. To help gain some objectivity, let's look from the perspective of the police department.

POLICE ARE PEOPLE and POLICE ARE HUMAN
•If you hit them they will hit you back.
•They make mistakes just like anybody else.
•There are good cops and bad cops.

I had a lady come to my office crying about the fact that she and her husband had an argument and somebody called the police. When the police arrived the argument had been settled and the couple was fine. The officers talked with the couple to determine what had happened. One officer was satisfied and was ready to leave. The other officer insisted that he needed to remove the children from the home in the event of future violence. The officers were divided but the older officer insisted on taking the children out of the home.

There is a reason why people act the way they act. It was later discovered that the older officer had had personal problems with his wife and children earlier in life and his children had been removed for a time. Every time he was confronted with a situation where children were involved, he quickly removed the children from the situation regardless of how minor the violence was between parents. There will be times when you are confronted by a policeman who may not make the best judgment. Remember that they are human and subject to the same passions that all humans are subject to.

POLICE MAKE MISTAKES
When we watch TV or movies and there is a good guy and a bad guy, we get to see both sides at the same time. The camera will shift from what the criminal is doing to the police on their way to the crime. In real life, this is not the case. The police usually don't know who committed a crime. They know it could be anybody so they suspect everybody.

Blacks resent the fact that from the White perspective, many of us look the same. Well, to me Koreans and Japanese look the same. They resent that. I mean them no harm but my knowledge of them is limited. In some parts of the country, the police are very limited, and easily make mistakes identifying young Black men.

THEY ARE HINDERED

The laws of our land are written to protect us from the infringements of government. These laws trickle down to the local level and puts restrictions on the local police department. A criminal must be:
- Caught according to certain guidelines.
- Arrested according to certain guidelines.
- Has many loopholes to use to get off of the hook.

The police are frustrated when they risk their lives to arrest a criminal and see him on the streets the next day continuing to do his thing. The police know where the crack houses are but they cannot bust the crack houses without sufficient concrete evidence. This evidence is hard to get because witnesses don't want to testify against pushers.

POLICE ARE HESITANT

During their training period the police are shown pictures of fellow officers who were killed in the line of duty. These pictures are shown to encourage them to be very careful when approaching criminals.

Let me paint a picture of a typically dangerous situation. A young executive at the local bank has been having trouble with his wife and this has disturbed him deeply. He decides to go home and discuss the problem with her so that they can iron things out. When he goes home unannounced, he finds his wife and another man intimately involved. At that moment he snaps and all of his pent-up frustration comes out. He goes into his den, grabs his 38 and begins to chase the man that has just run out of his house. The first man gets in his car and takes off, the second man follows. Now, Officer Smith is sitting at the corner of 4th and Lexington during his morning shift. He notices the blue BMW going at a high rate of speed down Lexington and he engages in pursuit. He has no idea what is wrong. He just knows to be cautious. After two blocks the BMW pulls over, officer Smith and other Officers approach the car. Now what do you think happens next? You don't know, but you do know that if you were Officer Smith you would be hesitant because of the potential danger.

Police are also hesitant because whenever they have on a uniform they are a walking target for a criminal or any deranged person who happens to have a gun.

BECAUSE I REALIZE THIS I AM PATIENT WITH POLICE WHEN THEY TELL ME TO STAND STILL WHILE THEY CHECK ME OUT.

POLICE ARE HIRED

I taught elementary school for a while and it was a job I loved very much. I enjoyed the little children and wanted to impact their lives in a positive way. One day a parent pointed out to me that as a tax payer, he paid my salary. I never thought of it that way. I now realize that teachers, policemen, politicians and all public employees are hired by the public. So, if I hire them, why should I fear them. When I started viewing the policeman as a person that I pay who is there to help me and my city, my attitude about him changed.

Too many young people see themselves as detached and distant from the local police officer but that is not how a good police officer views you. They have a responsibility to protect you from others and sometimes from yourself. I suggest that you seek to develop the attitude of cooperation

198

with your local police department because in most cases they only want to serve you.

QUESTIONS
FOR INTROSPECTION AND DISCUSSION
(to make you think)

1. Do you know a policeman personally? ___Yes___No

2. Are you afraid of the police? ___Yes___No

3. Do you cooperate with them when they ask you questions or do you freeze up?_____

4. How has TV influenced your attitude about cops?_____
   _____

5. If you view policemen negatively, would you be willing to sit down and talk to a policeman to get to know him better? ___Yes___No If you would like to talk to a policeman, ask an adult to set up a meeting with one.

6. Would you consider being a policeman? ___Yes___No
   Why or why not?_____

APPLICABLE SCRIPTURES

Let every soul be subject unto the higher powers. For there is no power but of God: the powers that be are ordained of God. Whosoever therefore resisteth the power, resisteth the ordinance of God: and they that resist shall receive to themselves damnation. For rulers are not a terror to good works, but to the evil. Wilt thou then not be afraid of the power? Do that which is good, and thou shalt have praise of the same:

Romans 13:1-3

Put them in mind to be subject to principalities and powers, to obey magistrates, to be ready to every good work,

Titus 3:1

Submit yourselves to every ordinance of man for the Lord's sake: whether it be to the king, as supreme; Or unto governors, as unto them that are sent by him for the punishment of evildoers, and for the praise of them that do well. For so is the will of God, that with well-doing ye may put to silence the ignorance of foolish men:

I Peter 2:13-15

A soft answer turneth away wrath: but grievous words stir up anger.

Proverbs 15:1

He that refuseth instruction despiseth his own soul: but he that heareth reproof getteth understanding.

Proverbs 15:32

PART SEVEN

FAITH'S FOUNDATION

CHAPTER TWENTY FOUR

Understanding The Certainty Of Change
(And Preparing For It)

ONE OF THE PROBLEMS OF BEING YOUNG IS that you have never been any older than you are. This is a problem for everyone, not just for young people. I am sure that you can remember anticipating a birthday or a time when you would graduate from one level to another. From elementary to Jr. High, from Jr. High to High School or from a learners permit to a full-blown driver's license. In each case when you got to the new level you found out that it was not exactly what you thought it would be.

I would like to warn you that most of what will happen in your future will be different from what you expect it to be.

The reason it is different is that young men have limited life experience. In other words they have not lived long enough to know experientially the results of certain behavior. Most men in thie forties can from experience tell men in their twenties: "If I only knew then what I know now." They have experience now that they didn't have then. I want you to consider the benefits of counseling, talking to and listening to those who are older than you are. The life experience of older men can save you MANY headaches.

The young men of our generation are missing dialogue with the elders which is one of the most stabilizing benefits that other generations have had.

In the African tradition, the Griot (elder in the village who knew wisdom and history) passed it on to the younger generation. In the Biblical tradition, the first manuscripts with God's wisdom were delivered over 4,000 years ago. Men have sought wisdom through God's word and through the elders. There is no new wisdom and no new way to get it but through God and the elders. A man who counsels exclusively with his homeys and himself is a FOOL.

I want to discuss some areas in your life that you should be willing to expose to the wisdom of your elders and counsellors.

1. BECAUSE OF YOUR LIMITED KNOWLEDGE OF THE FUTURE, AND THE CERTAINTY OF CHANGE, YOUR VALUE SYSTEM SHOULD BE EXPOSED TO THE WISDOM OF YOUR COUNSELLORS.

Please note that every man has things that he values. Some things may be good and some may be bad. You need wisdom to determine what to add and subtract from your value system. Have you evaluated your value system? Your value system needs to be based on transcendent values. These are values that transcend culture, race, and time. Transcendent, because they originated from God.

2. BECAUSE OF YOUR LIMITED KNOWLEDGE OF THE FUTURE AND THE CERTAINTY OF CHANGE, WHAT YOU LEARNED IN YOUR ORIENTATION FAMILY SHOULD BE EXPOSED TO THE WISDOM OF YOUR COUNSELLORS.

When young adults move out of their parents home, they are challenged to deal with new discoveries they make on a daily basis. These discoveries involve the realization that in our homes we did some things that were rather backwards. You may be able to identify some of these things before you leave home. In any case, we are thrust out into a world not fully understanding how our orientation will fit into the larger society.

One of my daughters, at 2 years old, would bite people. Her mom and I would brush it off and grin because it was kinda cute. She only did it at home so we did not work hard enough to break her of that bad habit. We were visiting some friends in Chicago who had a three year old girl. My two year old daughter walked up to the three year old and took a bite and grinned waiting for the three year old to grin back and play like mom and dad. The three year old didn't grin but she said to herself: "I know how to do that." The three year old then bit my daughter back! My daughter was traumatized because no one had ever bitten her back... Welcome to the real world.

I submit that your home shelters you from many elements of the real world. When you enter the larger world you are exposed to different ways of doing things. When you discover a truth or way of doing things that is better than what you learned at home, you need to make this new behavior a new habit. Once you start growing up, you need to ask yourself these questions:

- What is it that I need to know that my parents didn't teach me?
- How am I learning to compensate for short comings?
- Have I acknowledged that my parents taught me some things incorrectly.

A skill and discipline that each young man should develop is the art of REPARENTING ONE'S SELF. As you grow, you will discover that there are things you should have learned while you were elementary school age.

If you are mature enough to realize that you don't know something, then you are mature enough to see to it that you learn it.

If your parents neglected to teach you that:
>   A. Stealing is wrong;
>   B. Lying catches up with you;
>   C. You reap what you Sow;
>   D. You should do your home work;
>   E. Fast girls ain't NO good for you;
>   F. You ought to get out of that bed and do something constructive;
>   G. Everybody's not your friend; and

>   H. Your attitude will take you a long way, you need to learn these things.

If you were not taught these principles or many other basic truths, then as soon you become aware of them, you need to teach yourself or reparent yourself.

3. BECAUSE OF YOUR LIMITED KNOWLEDGE OF THE FUTURE, AND THE CERTAINTY OF CHANGE, YOUR SOCIALIZATION SKILLS SHOULD BE EXPOSED TO THE WISDOM OF YOUR COUNSELLORS.

My lovely wife is a singer of classical music. She has sung with some of the major symphony orchestras in this country. Occasionally, I accompany her to a concert. I am not extremely cultured and have very basic tastes.

Not too long ago she was invited to a dinner at a *SERIOUS* country club. I went along as her husband. As we took our seats I immediately knew that I was in trouble. On the table before me was a knife, two spoons and three forks. One fork to eat my meat with, one for the salad and I had no idea what the other fork was for. Now, if you want to look foolish at the country club all you have to do is to use the wrong fork at the wrong time. My wife was gracious enough to very discretely point to the right fork at the right time and saved me from looking out-classed.

Many young people want to better themselves but they have not accepted the fact that if you want to operate in bigger circles you must learn some new things. If you want to go places you must be willing to learn about the acceptable social skills of the larger culture. The President of the United States has people who are specially trained to make sure that he conducts himself properly when he is around people from other cultures. I suggest that we seek to behave in a culturally appropriate way.

4. BECAUSE OF YOUR LIMITED KNOWLEDGE OF THE FUTURE AND THE CERTAINTY OF CHANGE, YOUR ATTITUDES TOWARD WOMEN SHOULD BE EXPOSED TO THE WISDOM OF YOUR COUNSELLORS. You must be careful with what you say to yourself regarding women. What you say to yourself regarding women will develop into your attitude about women.

A. Never seek to use women for your own personal pleasure. If you use them it only **guarantees** that you will be used by someone else. What is worse is that it may come back on your children later in life. The principle here is you reap what you sow. Sow the wind and it will come back as a tornado.

B. Seek a healthy, safe Biblical attitude about women.

The elder women as mothers; the younger as sisters, with all purity.

I Timothy 5:2

This scripture provides safe guidelines for young men when it comes to their approach to women.

C. Remember that to have sex with a woman creates a bond that will never be completely broken. You will carry that memory for years to come. To have sex with a woman is to steal from her future husband.

5. BECAUSE OF YOUR LIMITED KNOWLEDGE OF THE FUTURE AND THE CERTAINTY OF CHANGE, YOU SHOULD STRIVE FOR PERSONAL EXCELLENCE with the help of your counsellors.

A. Never compare yourself with other men. To do so is unfair because we are all unique when it comes to gifts and talents. Use standards as the yardstick for improvement and seek to be better than you used to be.

B. Become a life-long learner. If you blew it in high school, determine to go back and get it right. If you are blowing it now, decide to stop and get it together. There are many things that you are too immature to deal with as you pass through life. Don't allow yourself to be defeated by any subject or obstacle that you were unable to conquer. Allow yourself to mature, then go back and try it again. The bottom line is that when you stop learning, you are basically brain dead. Resolve to become a life-long learner.

C. Associate with progressive people who are ahead of you. Think about this: The people that you hang with are the people that you will:

- Talk to.
- Listen to.
- Go places with.
- Spend money together.
- Party with.
- Go to Church with.
- Become friends with.

What is important to them, will become important to you. My point is that you are influenced by the folks you hang with. **THERE IS NO SUCH THING AS INNOCENTLY HANGING WITH PEOPLE WHO DON'T SHARE YOUR GOALS.**

A drug addict who was living on the streets and eating out of a McDonald's dumpster, sat in my office and told me that "YOU CAN'T HANG WITH THE COOLIE BOYS AND DON'T DO DOPE." So, if you associate with people who are not only talking about doing something but are actually doing what they are talking about doing, your attempts to be successful will be aided by their esence. If, on the other hand, the people you hang with only talk about being progressive then you should be careful because they could weaken your excitement about getting ahead. If they make statements like "next year, I'm going to get back in school" and next year never comes, you should get a clue. You will be pulled up or down based upon who you hang with.

6. BECAUSE OF YOUR LIMITED KNOWLEDGE OF THE FUTURE, AND THE CERTAINTY OF CHANGE, YOU SHOULD DEVELOP A RELATIONSHIP WITH GOD WITH THE HELP OF YOUR COUNSELLORS.

God is there where you are right now. You can ignore

Him and choose to deal with Him at some future date. That does not diminish the fact that your moment to moment existence is in His hands.

A. God knows your purpose in this life. Many people search for the perfect career but they should first search for God's purpose for their life. Many young people come to the University of Illinois and study for four years, get a college diploma and with their diploma in hand tell you: "I don't know what I want to do with my life." This is called four wasted years and a lot of wasted money. This can be avoided if we would only get our direction from God. Now, I am sure that someone is thinking: "I don't want to be a preacher." Well, you don't have to be a preacher to find your purpose and serve God. God may choose for you to serve Him by teaching school, coaching soccer, being a housewife, a honest politician, fighting drugs in your neighborhood etc. It is a very simple procedure to say to God: **"Jesus, please lead me to your purpose for my life and strengthen me in it, for your glory, Amen."**

B. Only God can give you peace. Peace comes from knowing God. When you know God, you have faith in the fact that you are on a winning team which may occasionally lose a game but is guaranteed to make it through the playoffs and win the championship.

C. Realize that God controls the future. The quality of your future wife, job, home, children and happiness are all directly related to your present relationship with God. God sees the future, we only see today and can speculate about the future.

CHANGE IS INEVITABLE AND UNCERTAIN BUT WE CAN BE BETTER PREPARED BY CONSULTING WITH THOSE WHO HAVE EXPERIENCED LIFE.

QUESTIONS
FOR INTROSPECTION OR DISCUSSION
(to make you think)

1. Do you have plans for the future?_____

2. How detailed are your plans for the future?_____

3. Have your plans changed in the last five years?_____
_____

4. At your young age, have you locked yourself into a
   career?_____

5. At your young age, have you locked yourself into a
   relationship?_____

APPLICABLE SCRIPTURES

> *Boast not thyself of tomorrow; for thou knowest not what a day may bring forth.*
> *Proverbs 27:1*

> *Whereas ye know not what shall be on the morrow. For what is your life? It is even a vapour, that appeareth for a little time and then vanisheth away.*
> *James 4:14*

> *For all flesh is as grass, and all the glory of man as the flower of the grass. The grass withereth, and the flower thereof falleth away:*
> *I Peter 1:24*

Notes:_____

_____

_____

_____

_____

_____

_____

CHAPTER TWENTY FIVE

Is Jesus The Answer to Our Problems?

W ELL, I KNOW WHAT AIN'T THE ANSWER!

Drugs ain't the answer,
Getting **pregnant** ain't the answer,
Dysfunctional families ain't the answer,
Flunkin' out of school ain't the answer,
Black on Black **crime** ain't the answer,
White on Black **crime** ain't the answer,
Black on White **crime** ain't the answer,
Talkin' `bout what we **ain't** got ain't the answer,
Talkin' `bout what we **can't** do ain't the answer,
Knockin' ankles ain't the answer,
Watchin' **TV** ain't the answer,
Hangin' with folks who ain't goin' **no where** ain't the answer,
Violent rap music ain't the answer,
Sexually **abusive** rap music ain't the answer,
Giving in to peer pressure ain't the answer,
Dope ain't the answer,
Misdirected **anger** ain't the answer,
Passive-aggressive **behavior** ain't the answer,
Having more than one woman to boost your **ego** ain't the answer,
Back-**stabbing'** ain't the answer,
Mental **slavery** ain't the answer.

Every man is required to make a personal decision. He has to decide if Jesus was a lunatic, a liar or was He The

LORD! Every man, in the private chambers of his heart must make a decision that will determine his eternal destiny. Was Jesus a Pretender, a Phoney or was He The Potentate. Was he Demented and Dangerous or was He Deity? Some say He was effeminate some say he was enraged and others say that He was Emmanuel.

Many decisions that we make greatly affect others. This decision must be made alone and will have an eternal effect on the decision maker. Did Jesus really walk on the earth, witness to men and Wash away our sins?

I believe that Jesus did all of those things. I have personally worked through my doubts and see the reality of Jesus Christ as a historical person. As I searched my heart, the world and the Bible I found some truths that have led me to conclude that Jesus Christ is what He said He is in John 14:6 *"Jesus saith unto him, I am the way, the truth, and the life: no man cometh unto the Father, but by me."*
Let me share with you some of my reasons:

1. The Witness Of Nature

It is very difficult to look at the ocean, mountains, forests, and stars in the sky and not wonder about God. Throughout civilization, men have looked at nature and thought about God. This is what is called "Natural Revelation." It refers to what man sees of God in nature. With only natural revelation and no written book, men have always sought for God and concluded that God was there somewhere.

> *The heavens declare the glory of God; and the firmament showeth his handiwork.*
> *Psalm 19:1*

I will praise thee; for I am fearfully and wonderfully made: marvelous are thy works; and that my soul knoweth right well.

Psalm 139:14

2. The Witness Of History

The history of the world is full of the influence of Jesus Christ. Jesus Christ has a 2,000 year track record with the inhabitants of planet earth. It was not until the 1800's, during the Age of Enlightenment, that men started questioning the validity of the Biblical claims to Christ's authority. Also, when the Bible speaks of historical accounts, it is always 100% accurate. Biblical history corresponds with secular history.

In the Bible, there are books of history which chronicle in detail the events of secular history. The Bible has accurately predicted the rise and fall of kings, and kingdoms. The outcome of wars have been predicted before they were ever fought. NO OTHER RELIGIOUS BOOK even comes close to the Bible when it comes to historical accuracy.

3. The Witness Of Prophecy

Prophecy is the ability to predict something before it happens. When it comes to prophecy, there is **NO OTHER RELIGIOUS BOOK THAT EVEN COMES CLOSE TO BEING AS ACCURATE AS THE BIBLE! (not even close!)** The Bible has made thousands of predictions that have come true to the letter and there are more yet to be fulfilled.

The LORD of hosts hath sworn, saying, Surely as I have thought, so shall it come to pass; and as I have purposed, so shall it stand:

Isaiah 14:24

4. The Witness Of Science

The Bible is not a science book, but whenever the Bible touches on the subject of science it is 100% correct. For example: Men said that the world was flat, the Bible says that it is round in Ecclesiastes 1:6. In the 1700's, men let the blood out of a sick person to heal them. The person usually died before he got better. The Bible says that the life of a person is in the blood according to Leviticus 17:11. In recent years much has been made about the fact that when two people have sex they share blood. Not only do they share blood but they share any diseases that may be present in their bodies. One person's body becomes part of the other person's body. The Bible states that when two people have sex they become one flesh according to I Corinthians 6:16. The examples are numerous where science has affirmed the Biblical position.

5. The Witness of His Impact on Society

No man in history has impacted our society like Jesus has. Our nation and the laws of this nation were modeled on the Biblical teachings. Marriage has found it's standards in the Bible. Historian Philip Schaff said, "This Jesus of Nazareth, without money and arms, conquered more millions than Alexander, Caesar, Mohammed, and Napoleon; without science and learning, He shed more light on things human and divine than all philosophers and scholars combined; without the eloquence of schools, He spoke such words of life as were never spoken before or since, and produced effects which lie beyond the reach of orator or poet; without writing a single line, He set more pens in motion, and furnished themes for more sermons, orations, discussions, learned volumes, works of art, and songs of praise, than the whole army of great men of ancient and modern times."

6. The Witness Of Changed Hearts

I feel that a changed heart is the greatest evidence that Jesus Christ is real and that He is the answer to our contemporary problems. I have lived long enough to see Jesus change the hearts of some men that I thought were too mean to be touched, even by God! Convicts, murderers, dope pushers, pimps, you name it, Jesus can touch them and they will change.

> *Therefore if any man be in Christ, he is a new creature: old things are passed away; behold, all things are become new.*
>
> *II Corinthians 5:17*

> *And Saul also went home to Gibeah; and there went with him a band of men, whose hearts God had touched.*
>
> *I Samuel 10:26*

Maybe you know someone who gave their life to Jesus and was changed so dramatically that everybody noticed. Believe me when I tell you that it happens everyday as men give their lives to Christ. The process of giving your life to Christ is very simple. Listen to the message given in these popular Scriptures:

> *For God so loved the world that He gave His only begotten Son that whosoever believeth on Him should not perish but have everlasting life.*
>
> *John 3:16*

> *Behold, I stand at the door, and knock: if any man hear my voice, and open the door, I will come in to him, and will sup with him, and he with me.*
>
> *Revelation 3:20*

> *That if thou shalt confess with thy mouth the Lord
> Jesus, and shalt believe in thine heart that God hath
> raised him from the dead, thou shalt be saved. For
> with the heart man believeth unto righteousness; and
> with the mouth confession is made unto salvation.*
> *Romans 10:9-10*

Reading these scriptures shows you that salvation is belief in Jesus Christ as Savior. Belief in your heart and confession with your mouth will get you saved. It is not based on a feeling but on the fact that Jesus is the door to the Father and heaven if we would only trust in Him.

A simple prayer like this will serve as a confession of faith: *Lord Jesus, I confess that I am a sinner and I need a Savior. Please forgive me of my sins, come live in my heart and receive me into your kingdom. In Jesus name I pray, Amen.* From this point, you grow in grace and the knowledge of the Lord, but everybody starts at the same place which is the confession of sins and the acknowledgment of Jesus as your Savior.

If you are confused about salvation or want to know more about it, seek out a pastor who will take the time to talk to you about it. If all else fails contact me and I will help you locate a pastor or church in your area who will help you.

QUESTIONS
FOR INTROSPECTION AND DISCUSSION
(to make you think)

1. Who do you believe that Jesus is?_____

_____

2. What is the basis for your belief?_____

_____

3. Has your belief ever been questioned? Yes_____ No_____

4. Have you ever doubted what you believe?
   Yes____ No____

5. Do you have questions about Jesus or salvation that no one has ever answered? Yes___ No___

6. If you have questions, what are they? _____

_____

7. Have you developed a relationship with someone who knows more about Jesus than you do? Yes___ No___

APPLICABLE SCRIPTURES

> *Let not your heart be troubled: ye believe in God, believe also in me. In my Father's house are many mansions: if it were not so, I would have told you. I go to prepare a place for you. And if I go and prepare a place for you, I will come again, and receive you unto myself; that where I am, there ye may be also. And whither I go ye know, and the way ye know. Thomas saith unto him, Lord, we know not whither thou goest; and how can we know the way? Jesus saith unto him, I am the way, the truth, and the life: no man cometh unto the Father, but by me.*
> *John 14:1-6*

Neither is their salvation in any other: for there is none other name under heaven given among men, whereby we must be saved.

Acts 4:12

For I delivered unto you first of all that which I also received, how that Christ died for our sins according to the Scriptures; And that he was buried, and that he rose again the third day according to the Scriptures: And that he was seen of Cephas, then of the twelve: After that, he was seen of above five hundred brethren at once; of whom the greater part remain unto this present, but some are fallen asleep.

I Corinthians 15:3-6

CHAPTER TWENTY SIX

Never Forget The Shoulders That You Stand On

I HAVE BEEN IMPACTED BY MANY MEN BUT primarily, I stand on the shoulders of two men. The first man was John Thomas Davis (1904-1993) my father. The second man upon whose shoulders I stand is Rev. B.J. Tatum, my pastor and mentor. I praise God for these men and others who have influenced my life. I am what I am because of their influence.

Every culture acknowledges the aged. In many African tribes, it is the elders who make decisions, arrange marriages, decide when to go to war and so forth. I am not suggesting that we go to those extremes, but I am suggesting that the wisdom and strength that young men receive from older men is invaluable.

The shoulders of an older man serve as a foundation that enables young men to rise to higher heights. The strong shoulders at home gives young men courage outside the home. It is the fact that there is a strong man who will fend for you that makes a difference. James Brown (The Godfather of Soul) says: "I'm a man, I'm a son of a man. If I don't get you, then Papa can."

I was fortunate to have a father until I was grown. As a grown man with children, there was still a strength I found from the fact that my father was only a few miles or a phone call away. Since he has passed, I have felt a sense of abandonment, confusion, and instability. Now that the physical shoulders are gone, I must stand on the strength that I received while they were here and the memories I have of having them.

Remembering the shoulders of our forefathers gives us a sense of connectedness to our past which gives us strength to face the trials of today. When I think of my father's struggles in racist America and how he survived, I am encouraged to stand and face the battles that face contemporary generation. I live in a different age than my father did yet my struggles are the same, and different. In spite of the differences between my father's decade and mine, the difference in specific details of the battles are small. The fact remains that it will take the same qualities of manhood to win in the present and future that it took to win in the past.

I can unequivocally say that the shoulders upon which I stand are the shoulders of undaunted manhood. I must say that my father never ran in the face of adversity. He was challenged to the outer limits of his strength, but he never ran. I will never forget this fact.

I feel that every young man needs to look in his past and find the strong shoulders in his family tree. Maybe your father's shoulders were not strong. If that is the case, then you should go back another generation to the shoulders of your grandfather. Don't be discouraged by the soft shoulders in your family tree, just keep looking until you find the strong ones and learn from them.

There is also a need to look outside of the family to find strong shoulders to stand on. As a Black man, I have my heroes. There have always been local Black men who were models in the community who served as heroes. I saw some of these men in Church, teachers in school or entrepreneurs in the Black neighborhood. When we look to the national level, we see the Black men who are making substantial contributions to society. As a young man, I revered Rev. Martin Luther King, Jr. as an example of real manhood. There were so many Blacks who were becoming firsts in prominent positions in our nation. I was very proud of these men. It was their shoulders that enabled me to go to the integrated school, go to the bank to get a loan, live where I could afford to live and stay in any motel in the country.

It is a terrible, terrible, terrible fact that many young Black men are forgetting that they are where they are because of the toil and sacrifice of others. Because of the sacrifice of my father, I was the first one in our family to get a college degree. I realize that I did not do it by myself, I reached that height only by standing on another Black man's shoulders. It is a fact that the young man who feels that he has made it and is making it alone is not aware of his roots nor does he have a general understanding of Black history.

I would like to make a few suggestions for you at this time regarding the shoulders that you stand on.

1. SEEK TO BECOME FULLY AWARE OF WHOSE SHOULDERS YOU STAND ON.

It is a mistake to take your support for granted. Many Black males who have fathers take them for granted and assume that they will always be there. To do this causes you to miss many opportunities for growth that may soon be gone. Take time to examine the strength you have received from men who are family members and those who are non-family members. Take time to examine their influence again for a new and fresh stream of energy, strength, and encouragement.

2. HONOR THOSE INDIVIDUALS OPENLY.

At this point in my life I speak freely about my father and others who are deceased. I also speak highly of the men who are living from whom I have derived strength and direction. My Pastor, Rev. B.J. Tatum has been a model for me of what it is to be a minister, husband and father. I have known him for fifteen years and during my early Christian years he was in front of me providing support and stability for my faltering feet and a source of protection from the dangers around me. Now that I am older and have experienced healthy growth as a result of his protection, preparation and prompting, we walk side by side fulfilling the ministry that God has given to our Church. I appreciate his strong shoulders and I thank him publicly and privately.

3. ACCEPT THEIR CHALLENGE TO SURPASS THEIR ACCOMPLISHMENTS.

The fact that a man provides shoulders for you is proof that he wants you to get ahead in life. You should see their effort as a challenge to exceed them even if they don't verbalize that fact. We should seek to surpass the accomplishments of our forefathers because we build upon their foundation.

4. DETERMINE TO BE STRONG SHOULDERS AND NOT SOFT SHOULDERS.

The fact of the matter is that if you are a man there will be many people who will need to derive strength from your strong shoulders. As a teenager, there are be small children who look up to you and want to be like you. When you become a man, children and women of all ages will look up to you for strength to help them face their struggles. Whether or not you become strong shoulders for those around you is a choice that you will consciously make. I encourage you to accept the challenge set by the high standards of our forefathers upon whose strong shoulders we stand.

QUESTIONS
FOR INTROSPECTION AND DISCUSSION
(to make you think)

1. Have you considered the fact that you stand on the shoulders of other Black men in history? Yes___ No___

2. Have you considered their impact on your life? Yes___ No___

3. Give the names of the men upon whose strong shoulders you stand._____

_____

4. Have you thanked them lately? Yes___ No___

5. Have you decided to become strong shoulders for those younger than you who are coming along? Yes___ No___

6. What actions are you taking to assure that you will be strong for others?_____

APPLICABLE SCRIPTURES

The just man walketh in his integrity: his children are blessed after him.

Proverbs 20:7

Praise ye the LORD. Blessed is the man that feareth the LORD, that delighteth greatly in his commandments. His seed shall be mighty upon the earth: the generation of the upright shall be blessed. Wealth and riches shall be in his house: and his righteousness endureth for ever.

Psalm 112: 1-3

Thou shalt not bow down thyself to them, nor serve them: for I the LORD thy God am a jealous God, visiting the iniquity of the fathers upon the children unto the third and fourth generation of them that hate me; And showing mercy unto thousands of them that love me, and keep my commandments.

Exodus 20:5-6

No man can enter into a strong man's house, and spoil his goods, except he will first bind the strong man; and then he will spoil his house.

Mark 3:27

A good man leaveth an inheritance to his children's children: and the wealth of the sinner is laid up for the just.

Proverbs 13:22

Thou shalt rise up before the hoary head, and honor the face of the old man, and fear thy God: I am the LORD.

Leviticus 19:32

Notes:_____

_____

_____

_____

_____

CHAPTER TWENTY SEVEN

Your Father Should Teach You How To Die

DEATH IS SOMETHING THAT OUR SOCIETY seeks to ban to funeral parlors and hospital emergency rooms. Society does not ban the violence that leads to death but it bans the idea of dealing with death. A wise father will address the issue of death with his son. It is important to come to grips with this concept early in life because it will have a great impact on the quality of life a young man will live.

I clearly remember the great concern I had each December as the calendar came closer and closer to the 25th. My parents had done a good job of impressing me with the fact that I'd better watch out, I'd better not pout, I'd better not cry I'm telling you why, because Santa Claus is coming to town. I confess that Santa Claus impacted my behavior. As a grown man, I am glad that I was also instructed regarding God. I was taught that there was a destination in life, there is a goal to be obtained and a crown to wear. I was clearly impacted by the fact that heaven was to be my ultimate goal.

When a father teaches a son that the ultimate goal in life is heaven, many problems have been prevented or curtailed before they happen. There are other benefits also:

1. Guidelines for behavior are set (the Ten Commandments)
2. The idea of metaphysical realities (spirit world) is implanted.
3. The child understands that there are forces more powerful than himself.

    4. A father providing a spiritual example gives religion a strong image which is more acceptable to a young man.

    5. When a father strives for heaven it becomes a family affair.

    6. The goal of heaven will provide peace for a man at the time death.

My father's death was and is a form of comfort and assurance to me. My father loved the Lord and lived within the parameters of Godliness. When his hour came to leave this existence and start another, it came peacefully. The hour was a time of contradiction in which there was the pain involved when bodily systems shut down in death, yet at the same time there was a peace as this turbulent existence ended and the new eternal existence with God started.

There has been much written about out of body experiences and those who have approached the gates of heaven and returned. I submit that those experiences are as different from heaven as sitting in a airport lobby is from taking a flight on a 747.

There is a difference between the death of a Godly man and the death of a godless man. I have personally observed and know of many cases where men who lived Godless lives faced their hour of death. It is not a pleasant sight to watch a Godless person die. In some cases they heave, pant, fight, their eyes roll around in their head and in some cases they attempt to fight something. The Godly people that I have observed leaving this world, left peacefully. **If I had no other proof for the existence of God and heaven other than how men die, that would be enough.**

A personal relationship with Jesus gives you peace when you come to that helpless hour and with assurance you can rest in HIM. One of the greatest faith builders is the death of a loved one who believed in God and trusted Him calmly in their last hour. Let me make some suggestions for the young man who knows little about this subject:

1. REALIZE THAT ONE OF THE KEY POINTS OF CHRISTIANITY IS THAT JESUS CONQUERED DEATH.

All other religious leaders are dead and still in the grave. So, death for the Christian is not the ultimate thing to fear. We fear what we don't know and I know enough about death not to fear it.

2. A FUNERAL IS MORE REPRESENTATIVE OF LIFE THAN A PARTY IS.

If you really want to see life's greatest challenge, go to a funeral and you will see what each man ultimately faces.

3. YOU CAN OVERCOME YOUR FEAR OF DEATH AND DEAD PEOPLE.

There was a time in my life where the thought of death scared me to death.

When you are afraid of death it paralyzes your effectiveness.

Just think what would have happened if Martin Luther King, Jr., Malcolm X, or Abraham Lincoln would have been afraid of death? Their impact on society would have been diminished and we all would have suffered. You should adopt the attitude of facing the fear and proceeding to accomplish your goal even in the face of death.

229

4. AS SOON AS POSSIBLE, GET SOME LIFE INSURANCE.

They call it life insurance but it is really death insurance. It is very sad when someone dies and there is not enough money to bury them. Don't leave your loved ones with this responsibility. The price of a decent funeral varies in different parts of the country but you should have no less than $5,000.00 in insurance to cover burial expenses.

QUESTIONS
FOR INTROSPECTION AND DISCUSSION
(to make you think)

1. Tell the truth, shame the devil! Are you ready for death? Yes___ No___

2. Are you afraid to die? ___Yes___no

3. If you were to die today, what would be the most significant contribution that you would leave behind or for what would be remembered?_____

4. Have you trusted Jesus Christ to handle your entrance into heaven? ___Yes ___No If not, who have you trusted?

_____

5. Whose death has been most significant to you?_____

_____

6. How did that death change you?_____

_____

7. Do you understand that the death of Jesus was the most important death in history because it satisfied God's anger with all men? ___Yes ___No

APPLICABLE SCRIPTURES

And I say unto you my friend, Be not afraid of them that kill the body, and after that have no more that they can do.

Luke 12:4

Precious in the sight of the LORD is the death of his saints.

Psalm 116:15

But we see Jesus, who was made a little lower than the angels for the suffering of death, crowned with glory and honor; that he by the grace of God should taste death for every man.

Hebrews 2:9

It is better to go to the house of mourning, than to go to the house of feasting: for that is the end of all men; and the living will lay it to his heart.

Ecclesiastes 7:2

Yea, though I walk through the valley of the shadow of death, I will fear no evil: for thou art with me; thy rod and thy staff they comfort me.

Psalm 23:4

What man is he that liveth, and shall not see death? shall he deliver his soul from the hand of the grave? Selah.

Psalm 89:48

O death, where is thy sting? O grave, where is thy victory?

I Corinthians 15:55

CHAPTER TWENTY EIGHT

The Final Chapter

TO CONCLUDE OUR TIME TOGETHER, I WANT you to think very deeply and try to discover what significant needs you have that were NOT addressed in this book. What needs are there in your life that have an unhealthy amount of control over you and neither you, parent(s), teachers, preachers, or friends have been able to find a solution to the problem?

Remember, this book was not designed to address all possible problems and I am sure that there is a personal situation that you would like to have addressed. I want to encourage you to consider your situation a personal challenge that with the help of God you can overcome. Please continue to read books by Christian authors in that area where you need strength. I want to tell you from personal experience that with a concerted effort on your part and God's help you can overcome ANY obstacle.

Once you have determined the area in which you need to grow, your assignment is to do research on the topic by talking to older men about it and finding books written on it. After you have done that, share your findings with a mature male and get his response. Remember that the only problems that control you are the ones that you don't face up to.

APPLICABLE SCRIPTURES

> *I can do all things through Christ which strengtheneth me.*
> *Philippians 4:13*

> *Wisdom is the principle thing; therefore get wisdom: and with all thy getting get understanding.*
> *Proverbs 4:7*

Notes:_____

_____

_____

_____

_____

_____

_____

Other publications by Rev. Harold Davis

NEVER ALONE
Dating From The Biblical Perspective

A book designed to help young people order their private lives according to God's Word. "Never Alone" was prepared for young people who are late high school and college age though the principles included therein transcend age. This book is perfect for personal study or for a youth group.

To Order Your Copy
call
KJAC Publishing
at
1-800-268-5861
or write
KJAC Publishing
P.O. Box 111
Champaign, Il. 61824

Notes:_____

_____

_____

_____

_____

_____

_____

_____

_____

_____

_____

_____

_____

_____

_____

_____

_____

_____

_____

Notes:_____

Notes:_____